CAMBRIDGE Primary Science

Workbook 4

Fiona Baxter & Liz Dilley

CAMBRIDGE
UNIVERSITY PRESS

Shaftesbury Road, Cambridge CB2 8EA, United Kingdom

One Liberty Plaza, 20th Floor, New York, NY 10006, USA

477 Williamstown Road, Port Melbourne, VIC 3207, Australia

314–321, 3rd Floor, Plot 3, Splendor Forum, Jasola District Centre, New Delhi – 110025, India

103 Penang Road, #05-06/07, Visioncrest Commercial, Singapore 238467

Cambridge University Press is part of the University of Cambridge.

It furthers the University's mission by disseminating knowledge in the pursuit of education, learning and research at the highest international levels of excellence.

www.cambridge.org
Information on this title: www.cambridge.org/9781108742948

© Cambridge University Press & Assessment 2021

This publication is in copyright. Subject to statutory exception and to the provisions of relevant collective licensing agreements, no reproduction of any part may take place without the written permission of Cambridge University Press.

First published 2014

Second edition 2021

20

Printed in the Netherlands by Wilco BV

A catalogue record for this publication is available from the British Library

ISBN 978-1-108-74294-8 Paperback with Digital Access (1 Year)

Cambridge University Press has no responsibility for the persistence or accuracy of URLs for external or third-party internet websites referred to in this publication, and does not guarantee that any content on such websites is, or will remain, accurate or appropriate. Information regarding prices, travel timetables, and other factual information given in this work is correct at the time of first printing but Cambridge University Press does not guarantee the accuracy of such information thereafter.

Cambridge International copyright material in this publication is reproduced under licence and remains the intellectual property of Cambridge Assessment International Education.

The exercises in this Workbook have been written to cover the Biology, Chemistry, Physics, Earth and Space and any appropriate Thinking and Working Scientifically learning objectives from the Cambridge Primary Science curriculum framework (0097). Some Thinking and Working Scientifically learning objectives and the Science in Context learning objectives have not been covered in this Workbook.

NOTICE TO TEACHERS IN THE UK
It is illegal to reproduce any part of this work in material form (including photocopying and electronic storage) except under the following circumstances:
(i) where you are abiding by a licence granted to your school or institution by the Copyright Licensing Agency;
(ii) where no such licence exists, or where you wish to exceed the terms of a licence, and you have gained the written permission of Cambridge University Press;
(iii) where you are allowed to reproduce without permission under the provisions of Chapter 3 of the Copyright, Designs and Patents Act 1988, which covers, for example, the reproduction of short passages within certain types of educational anthology and reproduction for the purposes of setting examination questions.

Contents

1 Living things

1.1	Bones and skeletons	2
1.2	Why we need a skeleton	5
1.3	Skeletons and movement	9
1.4	Different kinds of skeletons	12
1.5	Medicines and infectious diseases	15

2 Energy

2.1	Energy around us	17
2.2	Energy transfers	20
2.3	Energy changes	25
2.4	Energy and living things	28

3 Materials

3.1	Materials, substances and particles	32
3.2	How do solids and liquids behave?	35
3.3	Melting and solidifying	39
3.4	Chemical reactions	44

4 Earth and its habitats

4.1	The structure of the Earth	48
4.2	Volcanoes	51
4.3	Earthquakes	54
4.4	Different habitats	57

Contents

5 Light

5.1	How we see things	61
5.2	Light travels in straight lines	64
5.3	Light reflects off different surfaces	67
5.4	Light in the solar system	70
5.5	Day and night	75
5.6	Investigating shadow lengths	78

6 Electricity

6.1	Which materials conduct electricity?	81
6.2	Does water conduct electricity?	85
6.3	Using conductors and insulators in electrical appliances	87
6.4	Switches	91
6.5	Changing the number of components in a circuit	94
	Acknowledgements	98

ID# How to use this book

This workbook provides questions for you to practise what you have learned in class. There is a topic to match each topic in your Learner's Book. Each topic contains the following sections:

Focus: these questions help you to master the basics

Practice: these questions help you to become more confident in using what you have learned

Challenge: these questions will make you think more deeply

Focus

1   Match the bones of the skeleton with their functions.
    Draw lines from the names of the bones to their function.
    Different bones can have the same function, or more than one function.

Bone	Function
Skull	Support
Ribs	Movement
Arm bone	Protection
Spine	

Practice

2   Read the text about skeletons and answer questions about what you have read.

> Our skeleton supports our body. It makes a strong frame inside the body. It gives our body shape and makes it firm. Our skeleton also protects organs inside the body.
>
> We grow and get bigger because our skeleton grows. We begin to grow at birth. Our bones get longer and thicker each year. When are about 18 to 20 years old, our bones stop growing.
>
> Sometimes we fall or have accidents and break our bones. A broken bone is called a fracture. Doctors take special photos called X-rays to see if a bone is broken or not. The broken ends of the bone slowly grow back together again.

Challenge

3   Match the skeletons with the animals they come from. Write the letter of each skeleton next to the name of the animal it comes from.

Animal	Skeleton
Bird	
Rabbit	
Frog	
Crocodile	

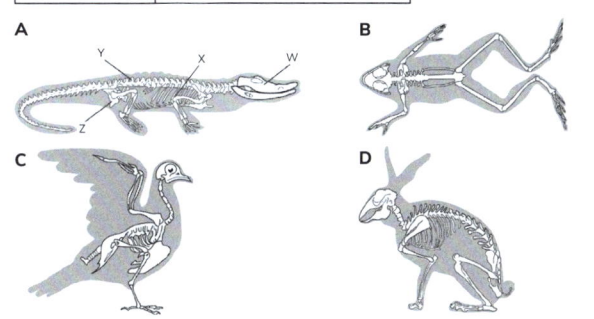

A   B   C   D

1 Living things

> 1.1 Bones and skeletons

Focus

1 Use the words in the word box to label the skeleton.

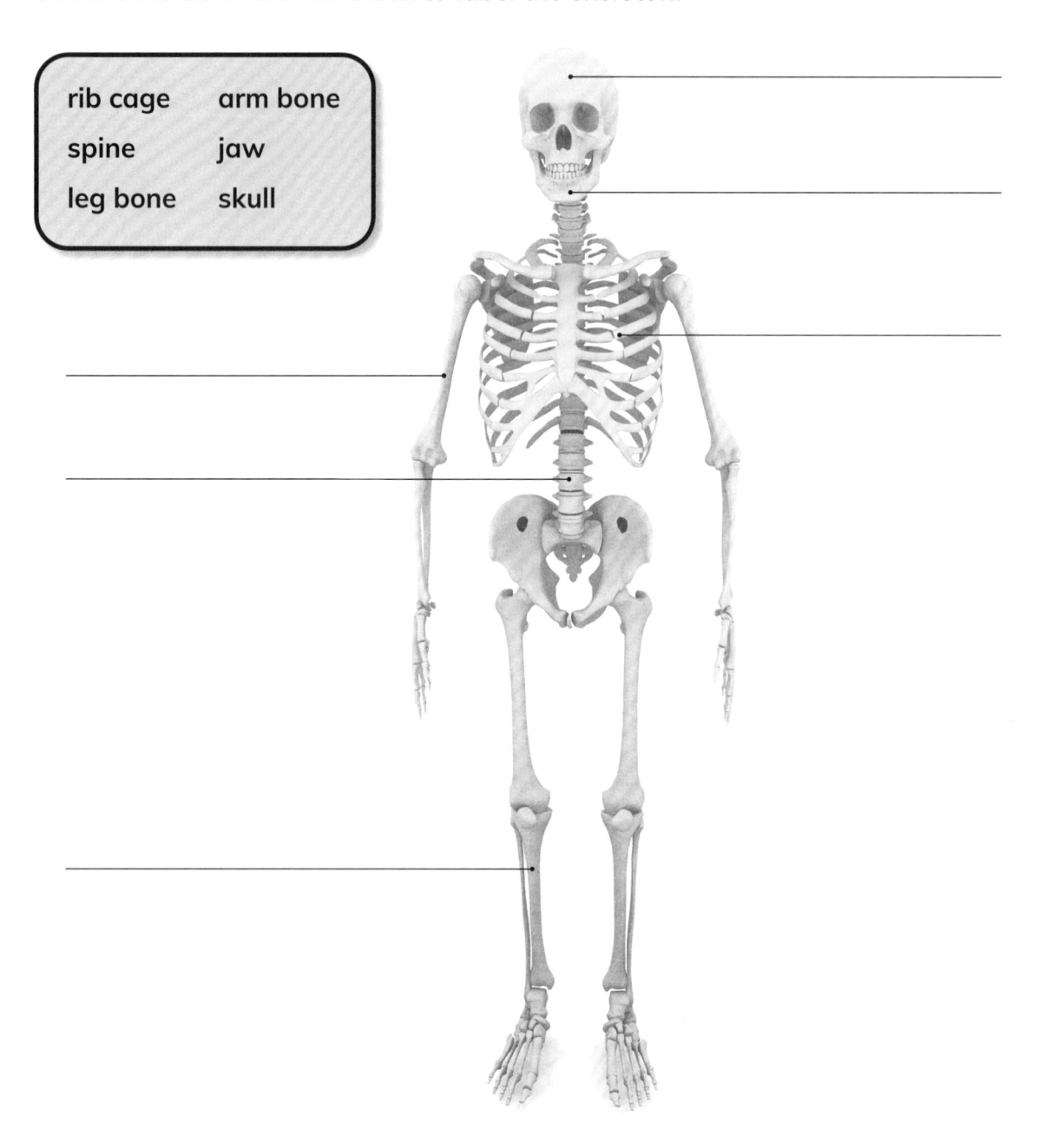

rib cage	arm bone
spine	jaw
leg bone	skull

1.1 Bones and skeletons

Practice

2   a   What are the bones of the head called?

    _____

    b   What are the bones of the chest called?

    _____

    c   What is the row of bones in our back called?

    _____

    d   Name the bone that moves when we chew food.

    _____

    e   Why do you think the bones of your skeleton are different shapes and sizes?

    _____

    _____

Challenge

3   Match the skeletons with the animals they come from.
    Write the letter of each skeleton next to the name of the animal it comes from.

Animal	Skeleton
Bird	
Rabbit	
Frog	
Crocodile	

3

1 Living things

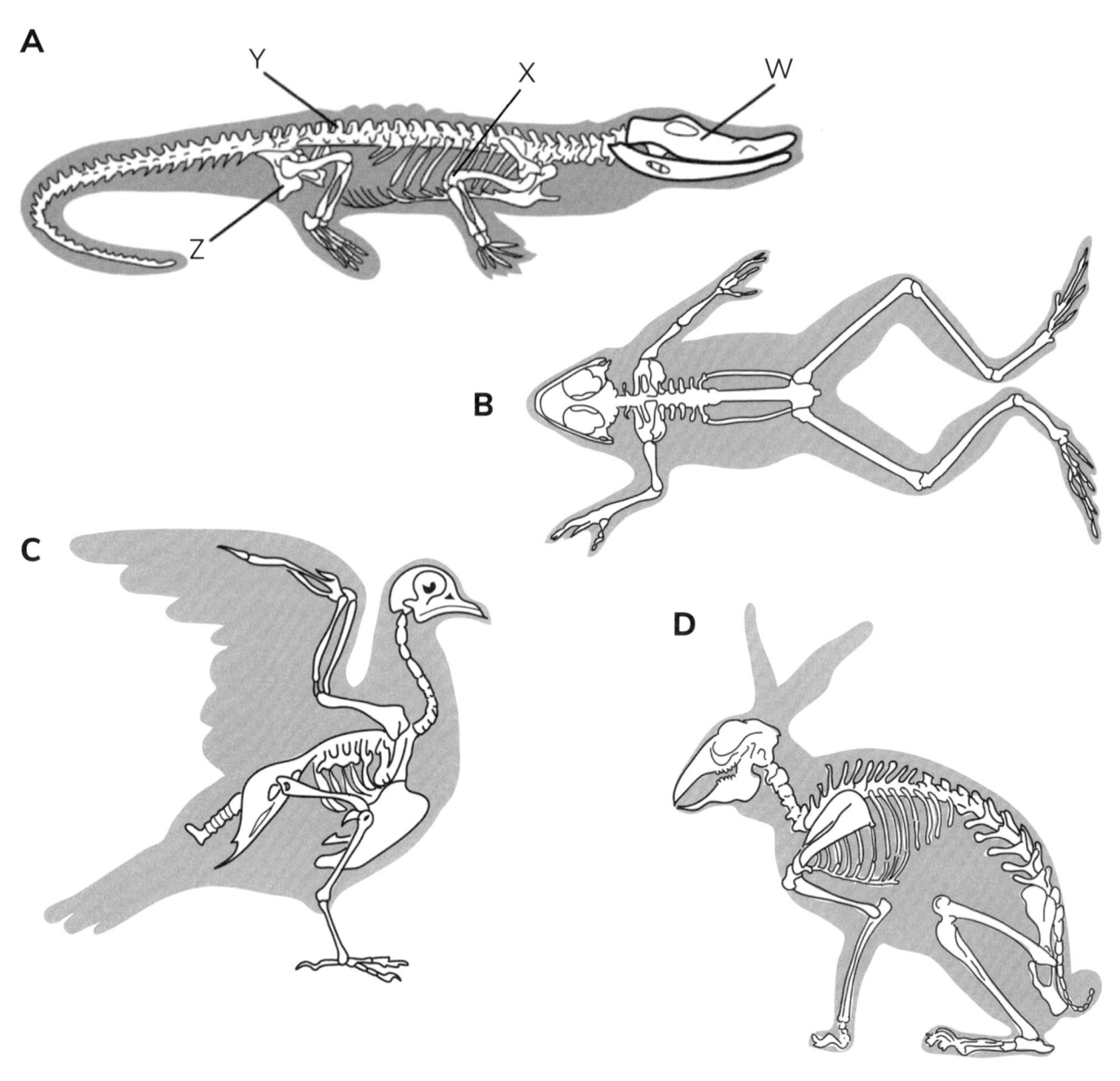

A
Y
X
W
Z

B

C

D

4   Name the parts on Skeleton A.

W is the _____

X is the _____

Y is the _____

Z is the _____

> 1.2 Why we need a skeleton

Focus

1 Match the bones of the skeleton with their functions.
 Draw lines from the names of the bones to their function.
 Different bones can have the same function, or more than one function.

Bone
Skull
Ribs
Arm bone
Spine

Function
Support
Movement
Protection

Practice

2 Read the text about skeletons and answer questions about what you have read.

> Our skeleton supports our body. It makes a strong frame inside the body. It gives our body shape and makes it firm. Our skeleton also protects organs inside the body.
>
> We grow and get bigger because our skeleton grows.
> We begin to grow at birth. Our bones get longer and thicker each year. When are about 18 to 20 years old, our bones stop growing.
>
> Sometimes we fall or have accidents and break our bones.
> A broken bone is called a fracture. Doctors take special photos called X-rays to see if a bone is broken or not. The broken ends of the bone slowly grow back together again.

1 Living things

a Name **three** reasons why a skeleton is important.

_____

_____

_____

b Explain what would happen to a baby if its skeleton did not grow.

_____

_____

c What is a fracture?

_____

d How can doctors find out if a bone is broken?

_____

e How do broken bones mend?

_____

_____

f Why do you think some animals with skeletons are very big, but animals like worms are usually small?

_____

_____

1.2 Why we need a skeleton

Challenge

3   In this exercise you will find information from a bar chart.

Nasreen measured the length of the upper arm bone of some people in her family. She drew this bar chart to show her results. Use the graph to answer the questions.

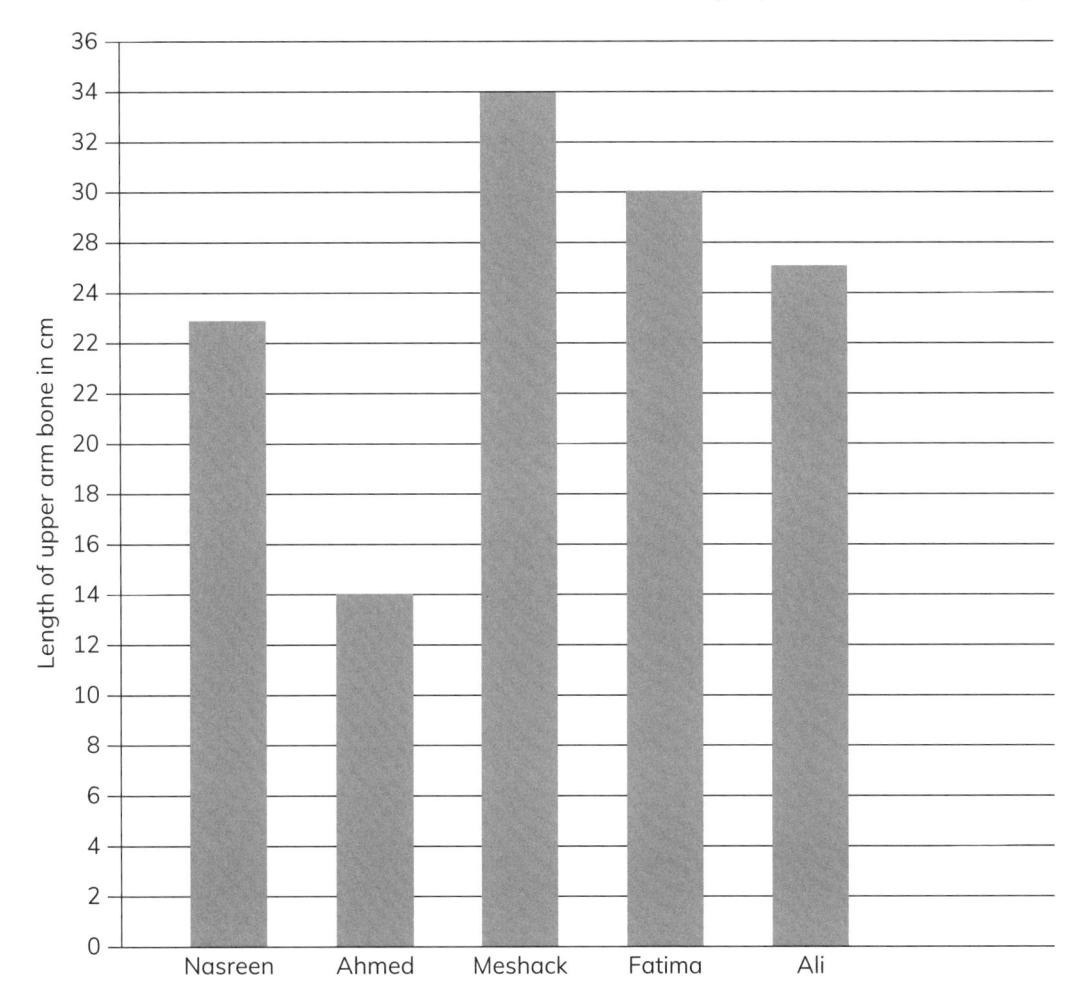

a   Who had the longest upper arm bone?

_____

b   How long is the shortest upper arm bone?

_____

1 Living things

c Nasreen's two brothers are Ahmed and Ali.
   Which brother is the oldest? Explain your answer.

   _____

   _____

d Put Nasreen and her brothers in age order. Explain your answer.

   _____

e Who are Nasreen's parents?

   _____

f Explain how you know this.

   _____

   _____

   _____

g Which function of the skeleton does the graph show?

   _____

h Nasreen has a baby sister, Meera.
   Predict the length of Meera's upper arm bone.
   Draw a new bar on the graph to show your prediction.

> 1.3 Skeletons and movement

Focus

1 Complete the sentences to explain how the muscles in your arm work. Use each of the words in the box once.

> pairs   shorter
> contracts longer
> relaxes

When I lift a weight, the muscle at the front of my arm

_____ and gets _____.

The muscle at the back of my arm _____

and gets _____. This shows that muscles

work in _____.

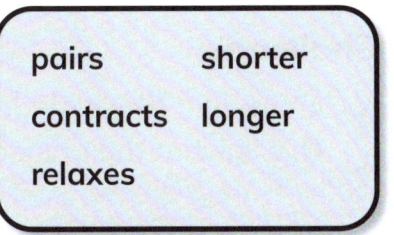

2 Label the drawing showing the changes in the arm muscles when you lower your arm.

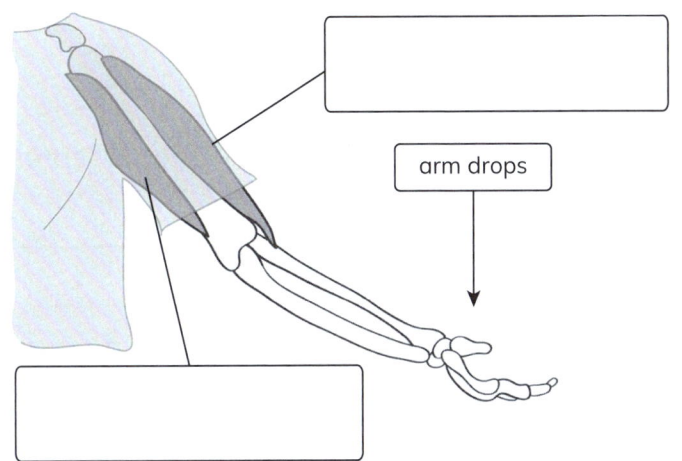

arm drops

Practice

3 Fill in the missing words to complete the sentences about how our muscles work.

Muscles work by _____ on the _____ they are joined to.

Muscles work in _____. When one muscle _____,

the other muscle _____. The muscle that contracts gets

_____. The muscle that relaxes gets _____.

1 Living things

4 Underline the word that makes each of the sentences true.

The muscle that is working **contracts/relaxes**.

The muscle that is resting **contracts/relaxes**.

Challenge

5 Amira and Jessie made a model to show how muscles work. This is what their model looked like.

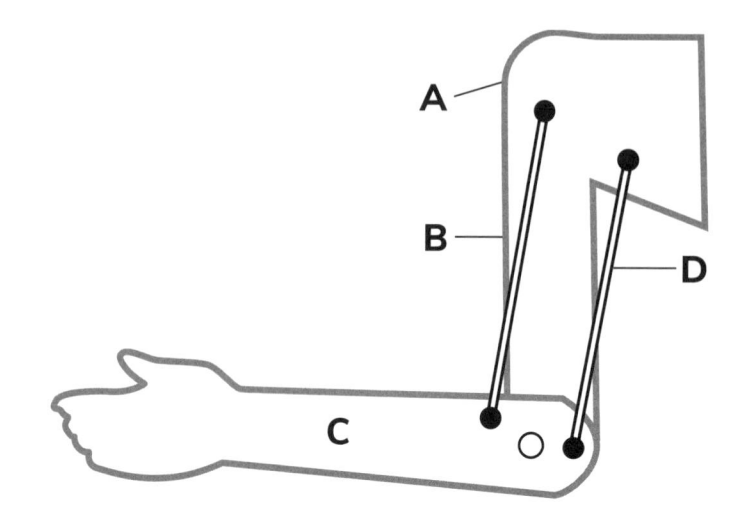

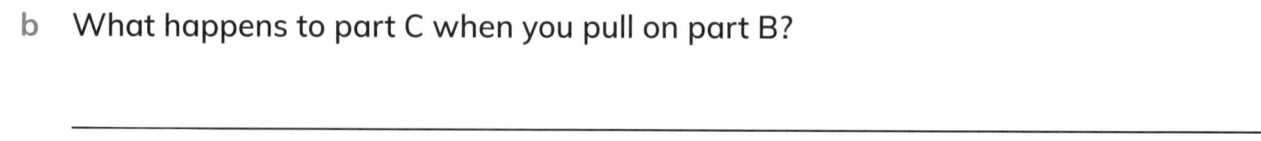

a Which part of the body does each part of the model represent?

A _____

B _____

C _____

D _____

b What happens to part C when you pull on part B?

_____

_____

1.3 Skeletons and movement

Make a drawing to show this.

c Underline the correct words in the following sentences to explain your drawing.

Part B **relaxes / contracts** and gets **shorter / longer**. Part B **pulls / pushes** on part C and makes it **drop / lift**.

1 Living things

> 1.4 Different kinds of skeletons

Focus

1 Look at the pictures. Which of the animals have a skeleton inside their body? Put a tick (✓) in the box below the picture of each animal that has a skeleton inside its body.

2 a Write the word for animals that have a backbone.

   _____

   b Write the word for animals that do not have a backbone.

   _____

   c Write the word for a type of skeleton found on the outside of an animal's body.

   _____

   d Which animals in the pictures have the type of skeleton you named in the previous question? Put a cross (✗) in the box under the picture of these animals.

1.4 Different kinds of skeletons

Practice

3 Look at the pictures of some invertebrates.

a Use the identification key to identify each animal.
Write the animal's name next to the correct letter from the key.

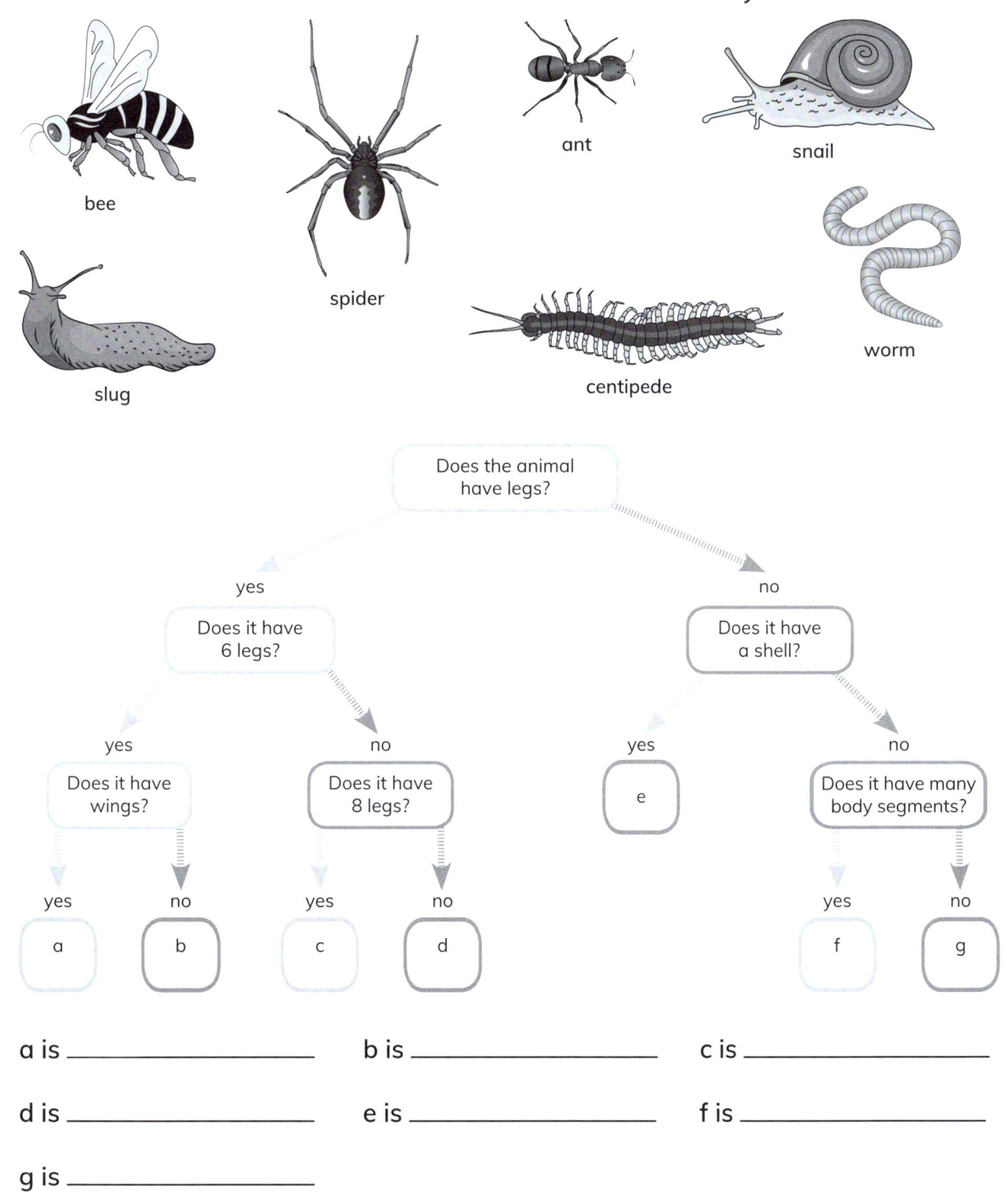

a is _____   b is _____   c is _____

d is _____   e is _____   f is _____

g is _____

1 Living things

b Why are all the animals in the key invertebrates?

_____

c Name a vertebrate that has

   legs and wings

   _____

   no legs and no wings.

   _____

Challenge

4 Write questions to complete the key to identify the animals in the pictures. We have written the first question for you.

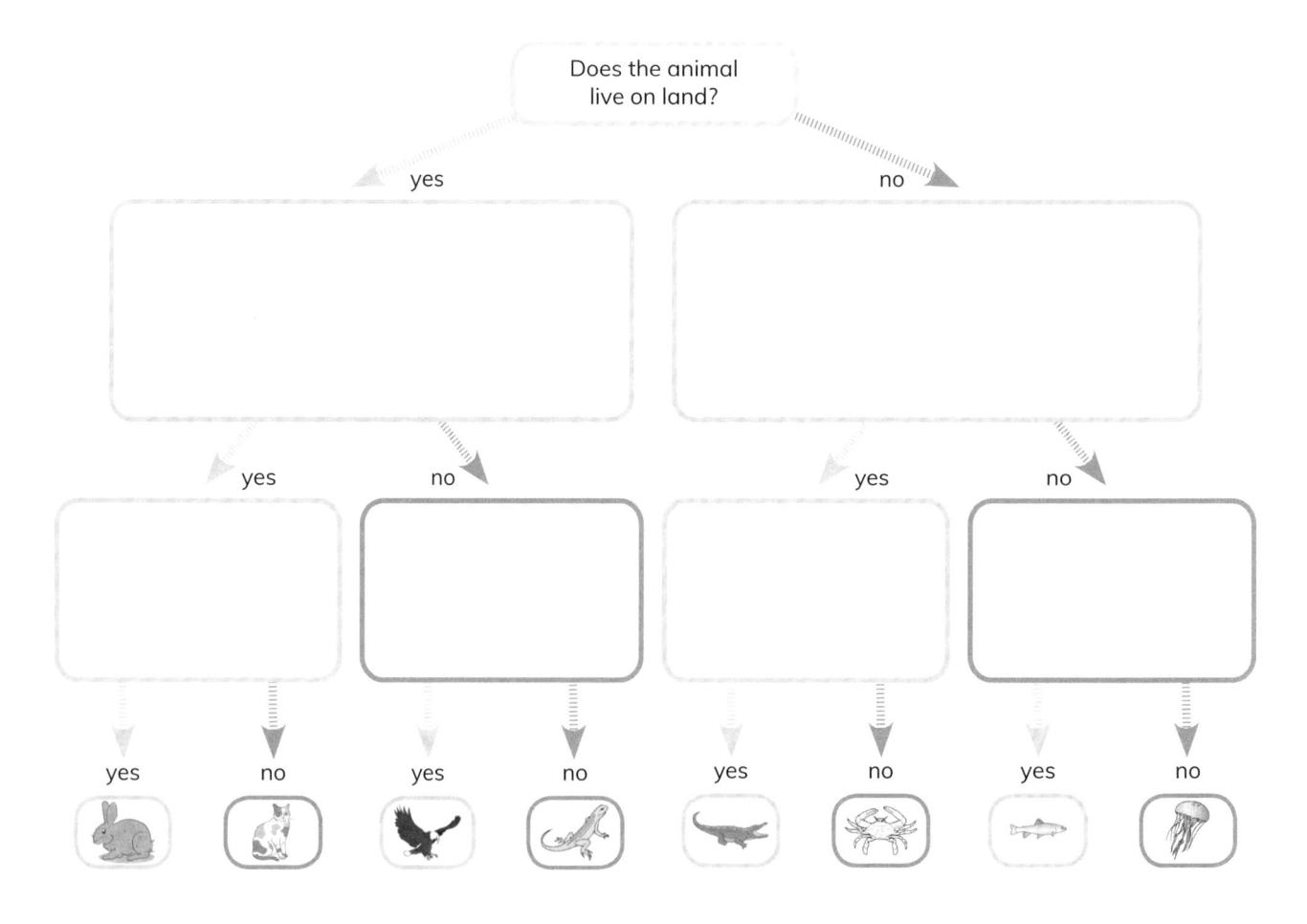

Does the animal live on land?

— yes → [ ]
— no → [ ]

yes → [ ]   no → [ ]   yes → [ ]   no → [ ]

yes: rabbit   no: cat   yes: eagle   no: lizard   yes: crocodile   no: crab   yes: fish   no: jellyfish

> 1.5 Medicines and infectious diseases

Focus

1 Mark each of these statements as either true ✓ or false ✗.

   A Medicines make us better when we are sick. ☐

   B Check with an adult before you take any medicines. ☐

   C Medicines cannot stop us from getting illnesses. ☐

   D Plants and animals can have infectious diseases. ☐

Practice

2 a Find **six** ways we take medicines in the word grid.
   Circle your answers.
   In the grid, some words are written from left-to-right, and some words are written from top-to-bottom.

i	n	j	e	c	t	i	o	n
n	w	e	r	t	a	n	i	o
h	a	s	d	f	b	h	n	l
a	c	b	r	u	l	l	t	h
l	e	d	i	n	e	m	m	d
e	v	f	p	q	t	d	e	f
r	u	r	k	l	g	o	n	u
m	i	x	t	u	r	e	t	p

1 Living things

b Which type of medicine in the word grid can prevent an illness?

_____

_____

c Which type of medicine in the word grid can help a person who has breathing problems?

_____

_____

Challenge

Marcus has a headache.
He finds some tablets in the bathroom.
He takes three tablets.

Speech bubble: My mother takes these, so they must be okay.

3 Marcus did not take this medicine safely.
   Write down **four** things that are unsafe about the way Marcus took this medicine.

_____

_____

_____

_____

2 Energy

> 2.1 Energy around us

Focus

1   Look at the pictures. Identify the form or forms of energy shown in each picture. Write your answers under the pictures.

a

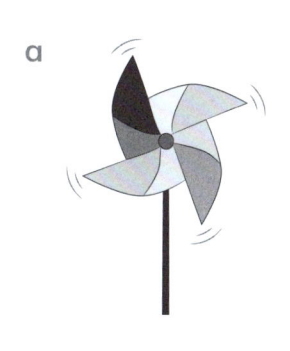

b

c

d

Practice

2   Decide which of the sentences about types of energy are true and which are false. Tick (✓) the boxes to show the true sentences.

2 Energy

		True	False
a	Things that do not move do not have energy.	☐	☐
b	Our bodies contain energy.	☐	☐
c	There is light energy in wind.	☐	☐
d	A stove gives off heat energy	☐	☐
e	A television set gives off movement energy	☐	☐
f	There is energy in running water.	☐	☐

3 Energy makes things change.
In each of the pictures, say how energy changes things.

a

_____

_____

b

_____

_____

c

_____

_____

d

_____

_____

2.1 Energy around us

Challenge

4 Unscramble the mixed-up words to name the forms of energy.

Then name something that has this form of energy.

Mixed-up word	Form of energy	Something that has this form of energy
ghitl		
veomtnem		
ehta		
nosdu		

5 Sofia threw a ball to Zara. The ball fell to the ground before it reached Zara.

 a Why was the ball able to move through the air?

 _____

 b Why did the ball not move far enough to reach Zara?

 _____

 c What can Sofia do to make the ball reach Zara? Say why.

 _____

 _____

2 Energy

> 2.2 Energy transfers

Focus

1 We can think of the way energy moves from one object to another object as an energy chain.

   Here is an example of an energy chain for drying washing in the Sun:

   the Sun ⟶ washing

   Complete the energy chains for the energy transfers in the pictures.

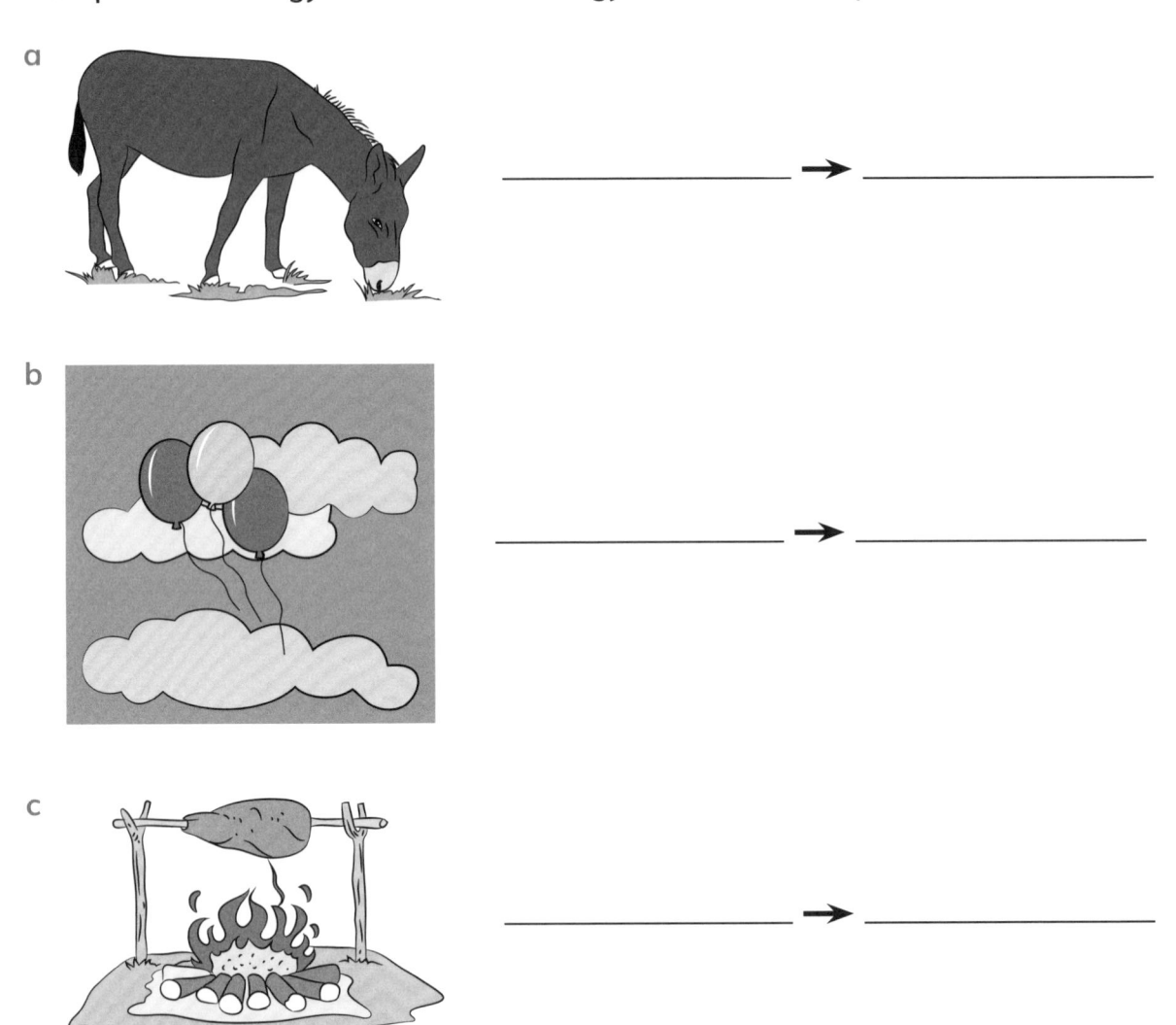

   a

   _____ ⟶ _____

   b

   _____ ⟶ _____

   c

   _____ ⟶ _____

2.2 Energy transfers

d

_____ → _____

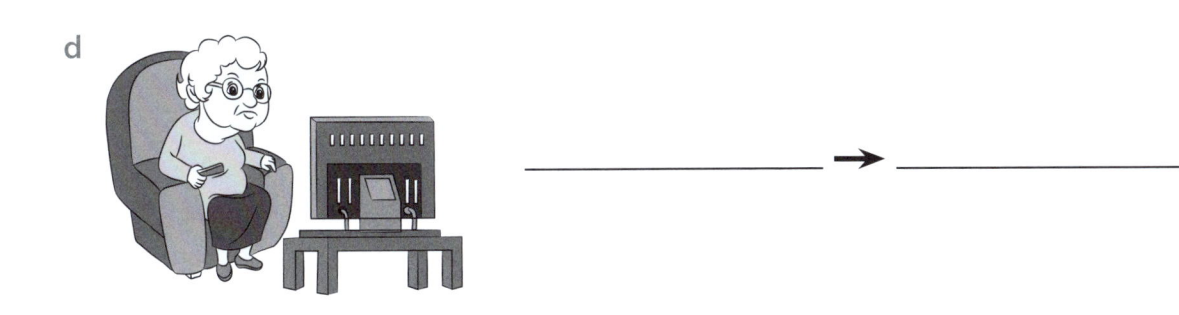

Practice

2 Why does a block of ice melt if you hold it in your hand?

_____

_____

3 The picture shows a spinning top toy.

   a What form of energy makes the toy work?

   _____

   _____

   b How does the energy make the toy work?
      Use the words 'energy' and 'transfer' in your answer.

   _____

   _____

21

2 Energy

4   The picture shows a solar water heater.

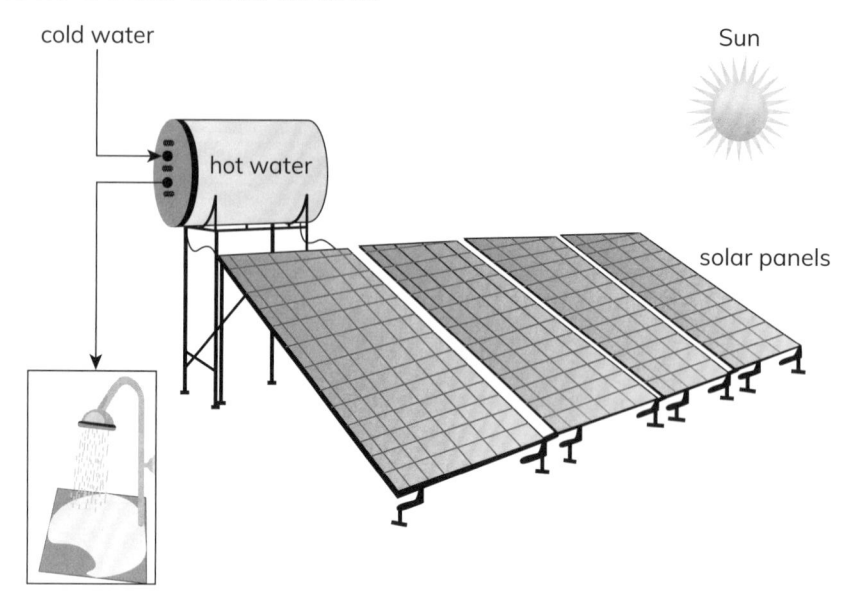

Draw an energy chain to show the energy transfers that happen to heat the water.

_____

Challenge

5   Class 4 investigated energy transfers.
They measured the time it took for a bead in a blob of petroleum jelly to fall off a spoon in hot water at different temperatures.

Here are their results.

Water temperature in °C	Time for bead to fall off in minutes
40	12
50	10
60	8
70	6
80	5
90	3
100	2

2.2 Energy transfers

Draw a dot-to-dot graph of the results.

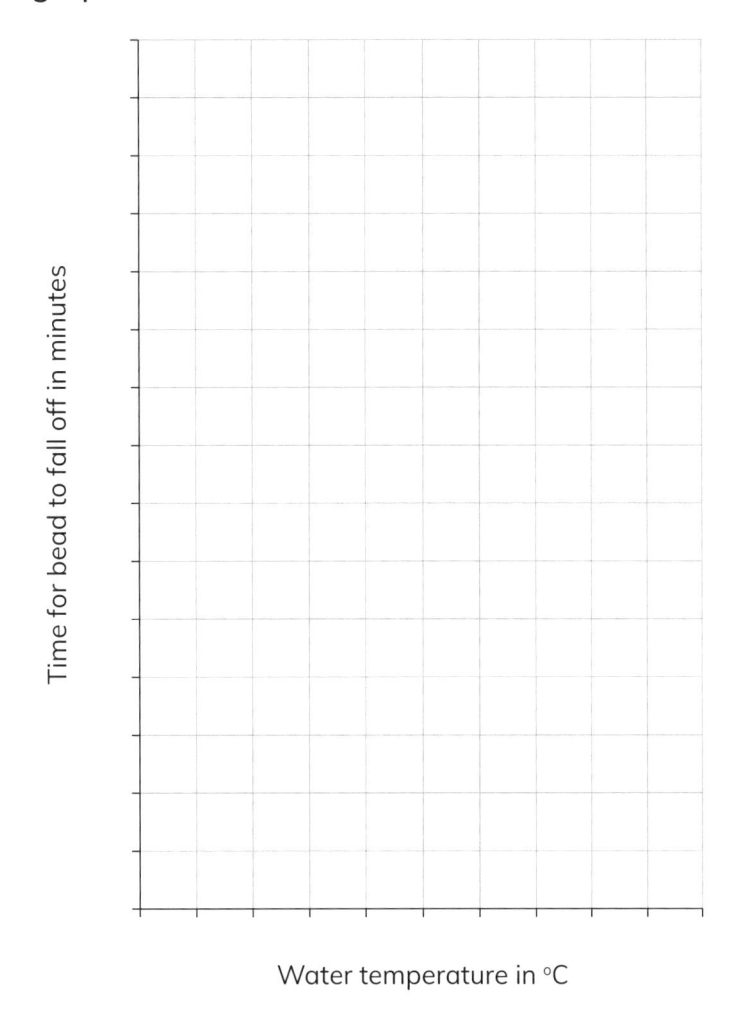

[Graph: y-axis labelled "Time for bead to fall off in minutes"; x-axis labelled "Water temperature in °C"]

a   Why did the bead fall off the spoon?

_____

b   At which temperature did the bead take the longest time to fall off the spoon?

_____

c   At which temperature did the bead fall off the spoon quickest?

_____

2 Energy

d Describe any pattern that you can see in the results.

_____

_____

_____

e Write a reason for the pattern.

_____

_____

_____

f Predict how much time it will take for the bead to fall off the spoon if the water temperature is 30 °C. Add this data point to your graph and join the dots.

> 2.3 Energy changes

Focus

1 Identify the energy changes in each of the pictures.
 Write the name of the form of energy in each of the boxes to show how energy changes form.

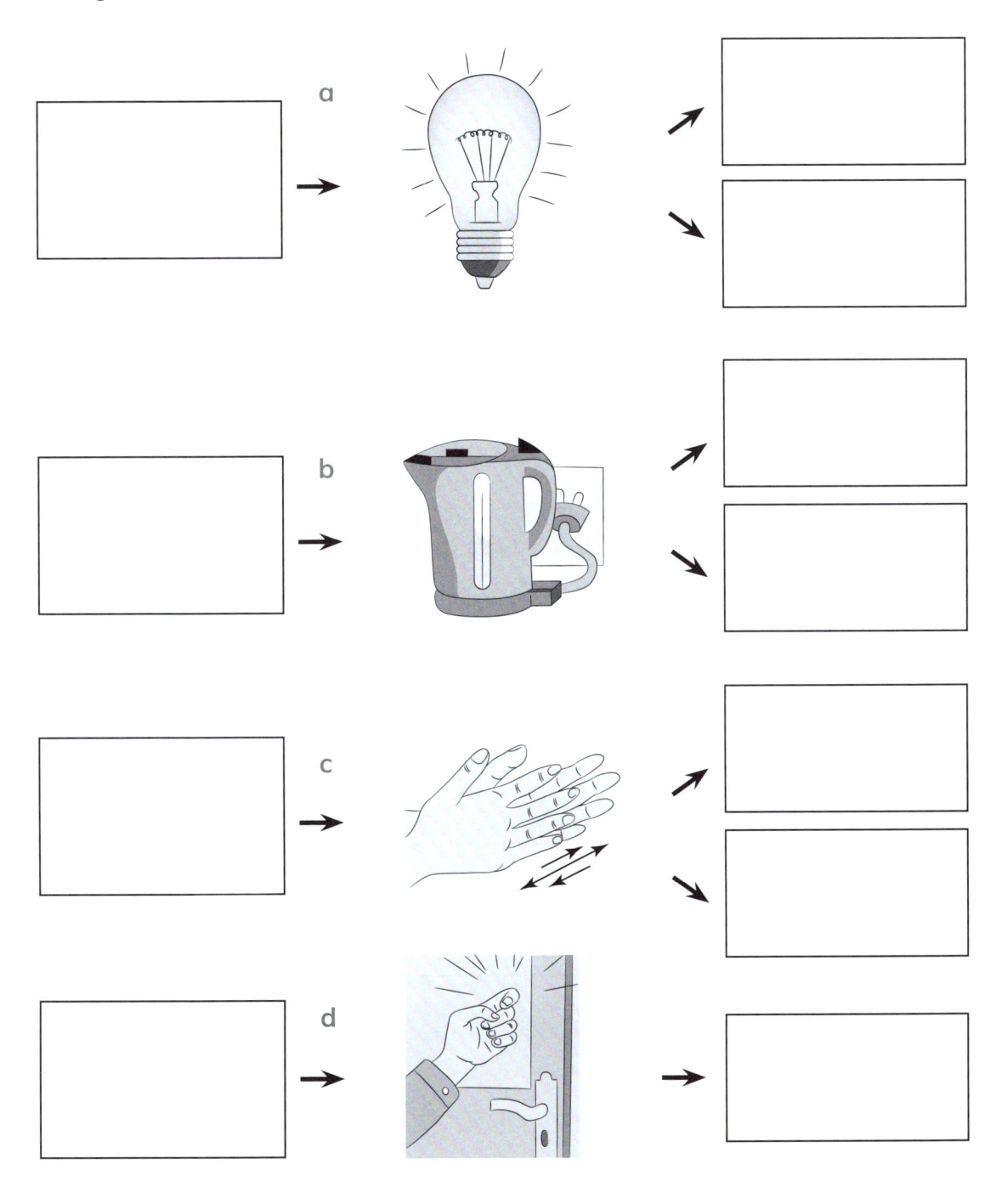

a (light bulb)

b (kettle)

c (hands rubbing)

d (hand on door handle)

2 Energy

Practice

2 Sometimes the form of energy changes when the energy is transferred.

Look at the pictures and fill in the table for each picture.

A

B

C

D

E

Picture	What form of energy is transferred?	Where does the energy go to?	Does the form of energy change? If so, how?
A			
B			
C			
D			
E			

2.3 Energy changes

Challenge

3   Read the sentences and then answer the questions.

> Vikal's classroom is cold and dark in winter. Before Vikal starts writing in his workbook, he rubs his hands together. The teacher switches on the light so the class can see the whiteboard better. The teacher shows the class a video on her computer. At break Vikal eats a banana. He then plays football with his friends until he hears the bell ring at the end of break.

   a   Why does Vikal rub his hands together?

   _____

   b   Draw an energy chain to show the energy change when he does this.

   _____

   c   Describe the energy change that makes the light work.

   _____

   d   Draw an energy chain to show the energy changes that happen in the teacher's computer.

   _____

   e   Where does Vikal get energy from to play football?

   _____

   f   Draw an energy chain of the energy changes that allow Vikal to kick the ball.

   _____

   g   Name the form of energy that tells Vikal that break has ended.

   _____

   h   Why is he able to hear the sound?

   _____

   _____

2 Energy

> 2.4 Energy and living things

Focus

1 The food chains below are not correct. Put the living things in each food chain in the right order and rewrite each food chain.

a snail ⟶ cabbage ⟶ duck

_____

b bird ⟶ caterpillar ⟶ leaf

_____

c lizard ⟶ corn ⟶ cat ⟶ locust

_____

d melon ⟶ eagle ⟶ snake ⟶ mouse

_____

Practice

2 Look at the pictures.

rabbit   plant   eagle   rat

2.4 Energy and living things

a Which living thing is a producer?

_____

b What do we call consumers that eat only plants?

_____

c Name the **two** consumers that eat plants.

_____

d Which animals are predators?

_____

e Which animals are prey for these predators?

_____

f Which animal could be an omnivore? Say why.

_____

g Draw a food chain for a producer and a consumer from the picture.

2 Energy

h   Draw a food chain for a producer, a predator and prey from the picture.

Challenge

3   Look at the drawing of a food chain below.

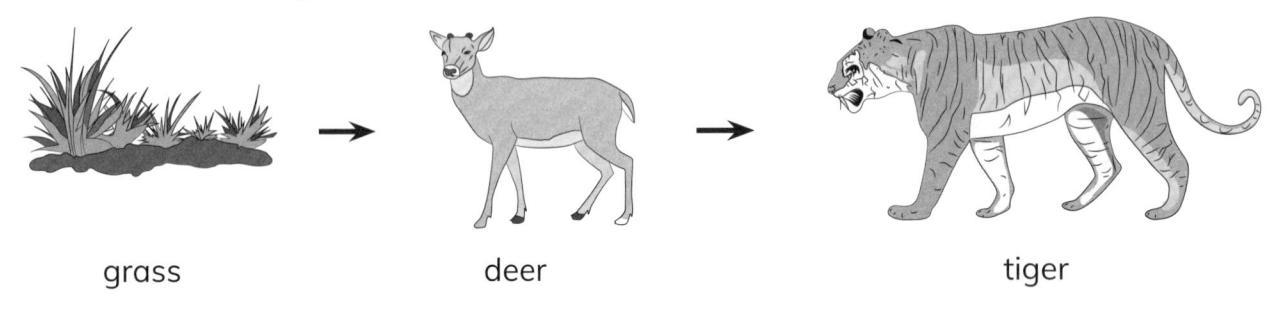

grass → deer → tiger

a   Why is the grass plant at the start of the food chain?

_____

b   How does the grass get its food?

_____

c   What do the arrows in the food chain show?

_____

_____

2.4 Energy and living things

   d Describe in your own words the information that the food chain drawing shows.

   _____

   _____

   e In this food chain, will the organisms always be in the same order?
      Say why or why not.

   _____

   _____

4 Bears are omnivores that live in the same forests as tigers.

   a What is an omnivore?

   _____

   b Add a bear to the food chain. Draw the new food chain.

3 Materials

> 3.1 Materials, substances and particles

Focus

1 Decide if each of the statements below describes a solid or a liquid. Write the word 'solid' or liquid' next to each statement.

   a   It has no fixed shape and can flow. _____

   b   It has a fixed shape and cannot be squashed. _____

   c   Its particles move very little. _____

   d   Its particles move around each other. _____

   e   Its particles are quite close together. _____

   f   Its particles are very close together. _____

Practice

2   Imagine that you have 10 particles of matter.
    In the boxes, draw the arrangement of the particles in:

   a   a solid
   b   a liquid.

   a   solid

   b   liquid

3.1 Materials, substances and particles

3 Choose words from the word box to complete the following sentences. You will not use all the words and you will use some words twice.

> solids   liquids   shake   shape   tightly
> loosely   spread   move   particles

All substances are made of _____.

_____ have a fixed _____ due to _____ packed _____ which _____ in a fixed position.

_____ can _____ and take on the _____ of their container.

Challenge

4 The drawings show how scientists think the particles are arranged in a solid and a liquid.

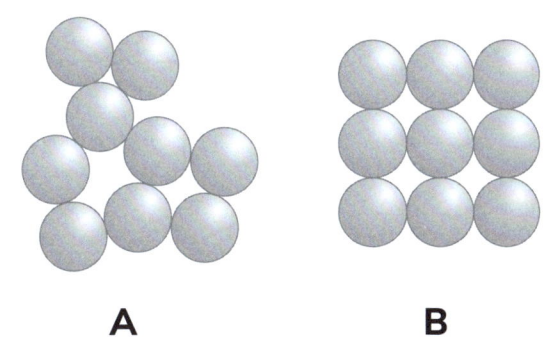

A   **B**

a Identify which drawing shows a solid and which drawing shows a liquid.

A _____

B _____

3 Materials

b Write **two** sentences about how the particles are arranged in drawing A.

_____

_____

c Write **two** sentences about how the particles are arranged in drawing B.

_____

_____

5 Draw a line to match the correct ending to each of the sentence starter below.

Sentence starters:

Endings:

| their particles can move quickly in all directions. |

a Solids have a fixed shape because …

| their particles do not move very much. |

b Liquids can change shape in some ways because …

| their particles can move around each other. |

> 3.2 How do solids and liquids behave?

Focus

1 Arun wants to show his sister that water can change shape.
   He chooses three different shaped containers.

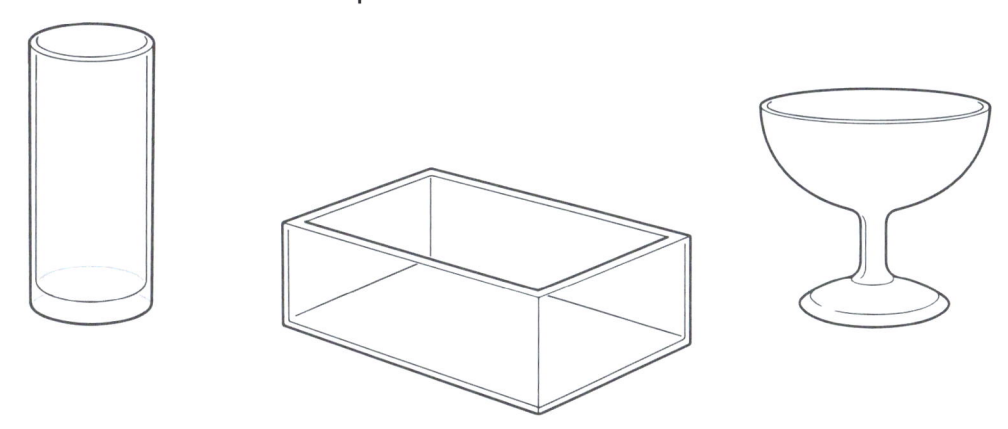

   He pours 250 ml water into each container.

   a Draw a line or lines onto each container to show where the water comes to when Arun pours it. Colour in the water.

   b Why did Arun pour the same amount of water into each container?

   _____

2 Complete these sentences to explain why the water changes shape when poured into the different containers. Use the words in the box.

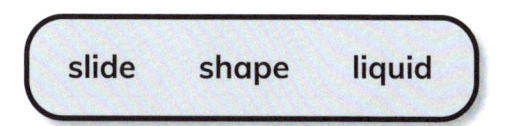

   slide   shape   liquid

   Particles in a _____ are close together, but they can

   _____ past each other and change places.

   Because of this liquids can change _____ easily.

3 Materials

3   a   Can Arun do the same demonstration with wood?

_____

b   Complete these sentences to explain your answer. Use the words in the box.

> shape   closely   positions

Particles in a solid are packed _____ together in fixed _____. They cannot change _____ easily.

Practice

4   Use the particle model to explain the difference in behaviour of solids and liquids.

_____

_____

_____

_____

5   Sand is a solid.

a   In what way does sand behave like a liquid?

_____

b   Why is sand able to behave like a liquid?

_____

_____

_____

c   Think of **two** more examples of solids that appear to behave like liquids.

_____

3.2 How do solids and liquids behave?

Challenge

6 Class 4 investigated how much time it took for different volumes of sand to flow through a funnel from one beaker into another beaker. These are their results.

Volume of sand in ml	Time taken for sand to flow in minutes
50	1
100	4
250	7
500	10

a Draw a graph of the results.

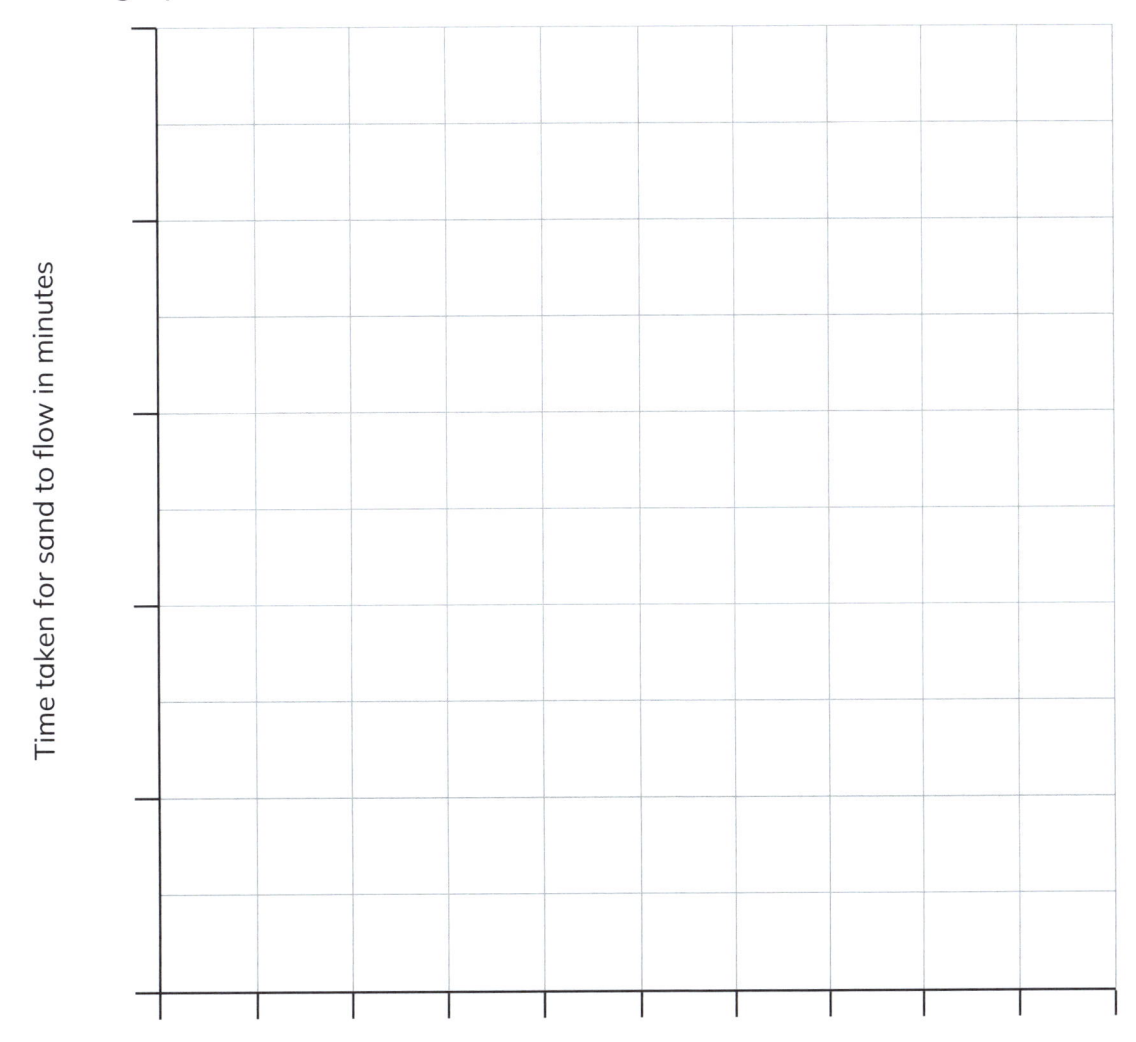

Time taken for sand to flow in minutes

Volume of sand in ml

3 Materials

b   Describe the pattern you see in the results.

_____

_____

c   Suggest **two** factors, other than the amount, that can affect how fast sand flows through the funnel.

_____

_____

d   Say in what ways these factors would affect the flow of the sand.

_____

_____

_____

> 3.3 Melting and solidifying

Focus

1 Solids and liquids are different states of materials and substances.

Sofia puts water into an ice tray. She puts the ice tray in the freezer.

a In what state is the water when she puts the ice tray into the freezer?

_____

b In what state will the water be when she takes the ice tray out of the freezer?

_____

c What must you do to the water for this change of state to take place?

_____

d Fill in this summary of the change of state:

water (_____state) $\xrightarrow{\text{cool}}$ ice (_____state)

3 Materials

2 Sofia puts butter into a pan. She heats the butter on the stove.

a In what state is the butter when she puts it in the pan?

_____

b In what state will the butter be after heating?

_____

c What is this change of state called?

_____

d Fill in this summary of the change of state:

butter (_____state) $\xrightarrow{\text{heat}}$ butter (_____state)

3.3 Melting and solidifying

Practice

3 Choose the correct answer to each of the questions.
   Draw a circle around the letter of the correct answer to each question.

   a When ice cream becomes liquid on hot day it is …
      A freezing
      B melting
      C soldifying
      D cooling

   b We can show the process of melting like this:
      A liquid + heat → solid
      B gas – heat → liquid
      C solid + heat → liquid
      D solid – heat → liquid

   c We can show the process of freezing like this:
      A liquid – heat → solid
      B gas + heat → liquid
      C solid + heat → liquid
      D gas – heat → solid

   d Solids melt because …
      A their particles gain energy and break away from the solid
      B their particles are not moving fast enough to stay in the solid
      C new liquid particles form when the solid is heated
      D solids cannot keep their shape when heated

   e The opposite of ice melting is …
      A flowing
      B thawing
      C cooling
      D solidifying

3 Materials

Challenge

4 Arun asked a question: Does ice melt faster in hot water or in cold water? He put an ice cube into beakers of water at different temperatures. He timed how long it took for the ice cube to melt in each beaker. Arun presented his results in a graph.

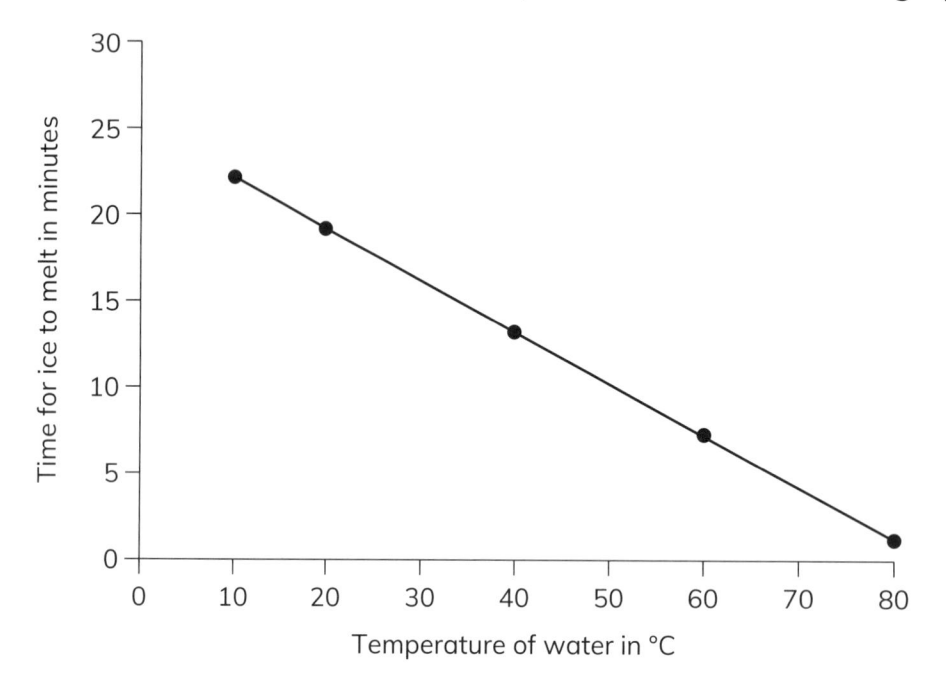

a At which temperature did the ice melt quickest? _____

b At which temperature did the ice take the longest time to melt? _____

c How much time did it take for the ice to melt at 40 °C? _____

d Suggest **two** ways that Arun could make his test fair.

_____

_____

e Write a conclusion for the investigation.

_____

_____

3.3 Melting and solidifying

f   Use the particle model to explain your conclusion.

_____

_____

_____

_____

g   Predict how the melting time would change if Arun crushed each ice cube before he put the ice in the water. Say why you think this. Think about energy transfers.

_____

_____

h   Suggest **two** ways that Arun could work safely in the investigation.

_____

_____

3 Materials

> 3.4 Chemical reactions

Focus

1 Look at the pictures and say if a chemical reaction has taken place or not. Circle the correct answer under each picture.

a

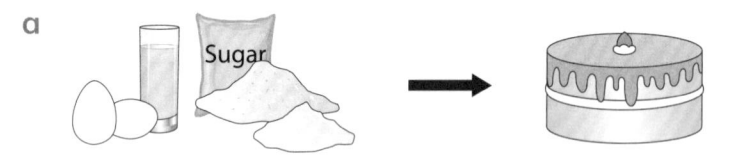

chemical reaction / no chemical reaction

b

chemical reaction / no chemical reaction

c

sand   limestone   soda ash   glass bottle

chemical reaction / no chemical reaction

d

nail   rusty nail

chemical reaction / no chemical reaction

e

sand   water

chemical reaction / no chemical reaction

3.4 Chemical reactions

Practice

2 Decide which of the sentences about chemical reactions are true and which are false. Tick (✓) the boxes to show the true sentences.

		True	False
a	Chemical reactions make new substances form.	☐	☐
b	When butter melts, it is a chemical reaction.	☐	☐
c	We cannot undo a chemical reaction.	☐	☐
d	Making concrete is a chemical reaction.	☐	☐
e	We need heat for chemical reactions to happen.	☐	☐
f	A chemical reaction can happen with only one substance.	☐	☐

3 Zara mixed baking powder with vinegar.
   The mixture started to bubble and fizz.

   a Did a chemical reaction take place? _____

   b How do you know this?

   _____

3 Materials

Challenge

4   Class 4 did an investigation on rusting. This is a drawing of their experiment.

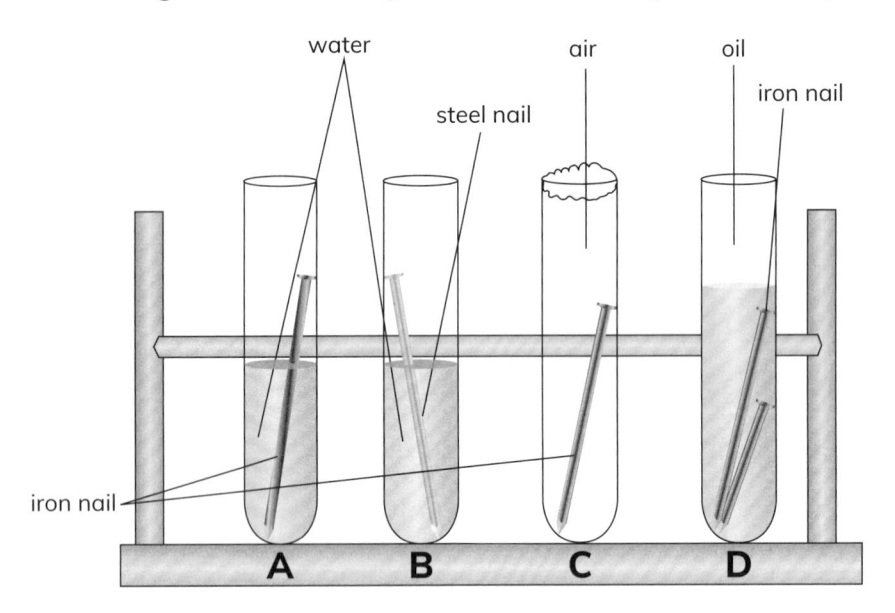

After two days they found that the nail in test tube A was rusted.
The nails in the test tubes B and C did not rust.
There was very little rust on the nail in test tube D.

a   What reacts with metal to form rust?

A _____

B _____

b   Suggest reasons for the results in test tubes A, C and D.

_____

_____

_____

_____

3.4 Chemical reactions

c Iron and steel are both metals.
   Why do think the steel nail did not rust? Suggest a question you could investigate.

   _____

d To make your test fair, which factors would you keep the same?

   _____

   _____

e Which factor would you change?

   _____

4 Earth and its habitats

> 4.1 The structure of the Earth

Focus

1 Choose the correct alternatives to complete the following sentences.

The **internal / external** structure of the Earth describes what is below the surface.

The Earth's crust is **thinner / thicker** below the oceans than below the land.

The outer core of the Earth is **solid / liquid**.

The core consists of **magma / metals**.

The mantle consists of **lava / magma**.

The Earth's crust is the **thickest / thinnest** layer of the Earth.

The temperature **decreases / increases** as you get closer to the centre of the Earth.

The **core / mantle** is the thickest layer of the Earth.

The inner core of the Earth is **solid / liquid**.

Magma is a **solid / liquid** material.

4.1 The structure of the Earth

Practice

2 a Complete this diagram of the internal structure of the Earth by labelling the four layers.

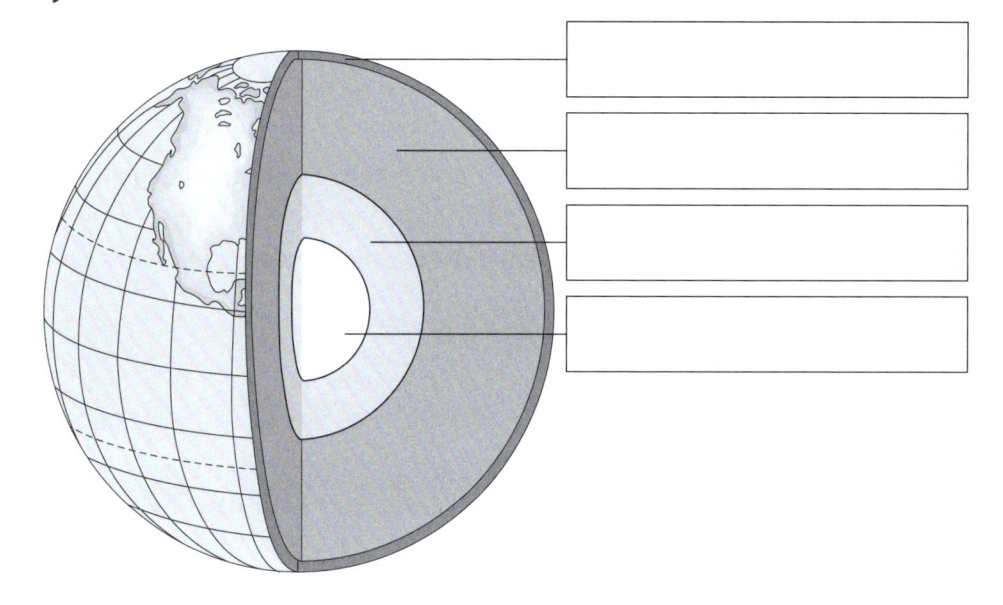

b Write down what material each layer consists of.

_____

_____

_____

_____

c Describe each layer as solid or liquid.

_____

_____

_____

_____

4 Earth and its habitats

Challenge

3 Read the text about the interior of the Earth and answer the questions below.

> Nobody has seen the interior of the Earth. So how do scientists know about the internal structure of the Earth?
>
> In the 1970s, scientists from the USSR decided to drill a hole deeper than anyone had ever done before. For the next 24 years, they drilled 12 km into the Earth's crust in the Kola Peninsula in northern Russia. The temperature at the bottom of the hole reached 180°C. This was too hot to continue drilling.
>
> The Russian scientists estimated that the distance to the centre of the Earth is nearly 6400 kilometres.
>
> Because it is impossible to drill a hole to the centre of the Earth, scientists have to use other ways to find out about the structure of the interior of the Earth. They use earthquake waves to tell them what the materials in the interior of the Earth are like. The waves travel through the Earth during and after an earthquake. The speed of the waves is affected by the hardness of material they pass through. These studies show that the outer core is liquid and the inner core is solid.

a How deep is the deepest hole ever drilled through the Earth's crust?

_____

b Why can people not make a deeper hole?

_____

c How did scientists discover that the inner core is solid and the outer core is liquid?

_____

_____

_____

> 4.2 Volcanoes

Focus

1 Fill in the missing words. Choose words from this list:

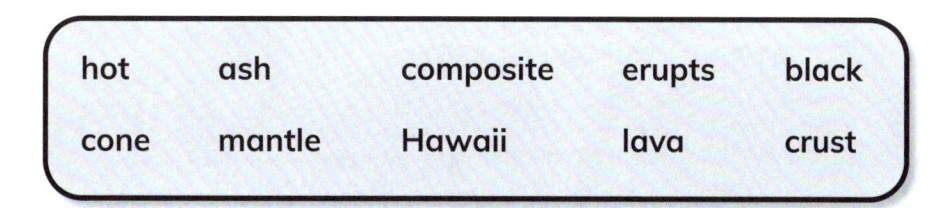

> hot   ash   composite   erupts   black
> cone   mantle   Hawaii   lava   crust

When a volcano _____, magma from the _____ comes

to the surface through a crack in the _____. When magma reaches

the surface it is called _____.

Sometimes lava and _____ come out of the volcano.

These materials build up to form a _____ shaped mountain called a

_____ volcano.

When the lava is very runny it moves quickly over the surface.

The islands of _____ were formed like this. The lava cools to form

_____ rocks.

4 Earth and its habitats

Practice

2 This map shows where there are volcanoes in the world.
   The black circles are volcanoes that erupt regularly.
   The white circles are old volcanoes that have not erupted for a long time.

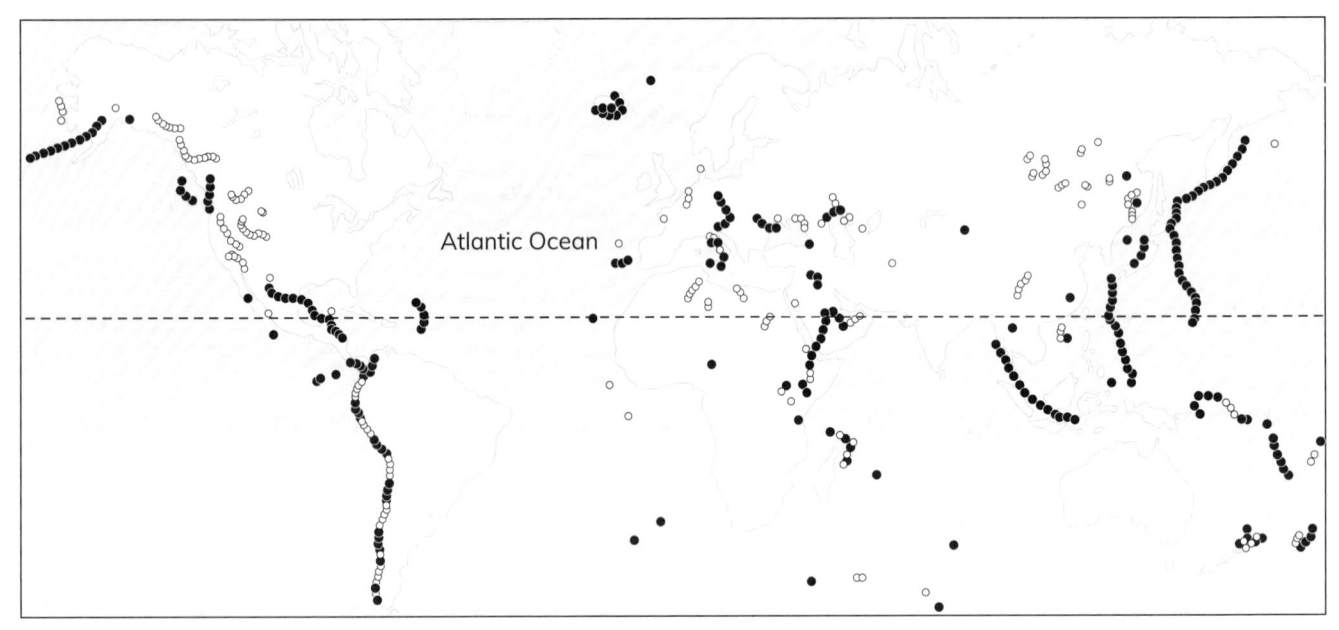

a Find the Pacific Ocean on the map.
   Use a coloured pen or pencil to draw in the Pacific Ring of Fire.

b Why is this area called the Pacific Ring of Fire?

_____

_____

c Why do some parts of the world have lots of volcanoes and other parts of the world have no volcanoes?

_____

_____

4.2 Volcanoes

Challenge

3   Read the sentences below.
    The sentences describe how a composite volcano erupts, but they are in the wrong order. Write numbers 1–6 next to the sentences so that the sentences describe events in the correct order.

   A A secondary cone develops on the side of the volcano. ☐

   B A crack develops in the Earth's crust and magma travels up the crack to the surface of the Earth. ☐

   C A mountain forms of alternate layers of lava and ash. ☐

   D Ash is hurled out of the volcano and forms a layer on the volcano. ☐

   E Lava flows out of the crater and down the sides of the volcano. ☐

   F A side vent forms and lava erupts on the side of the volcano. ☐

53

4 Earth and its habitats

> 4.3 Earthquakes

Focus

1 a Complete these sentences, which explain how earthquakes happen. Use these words:

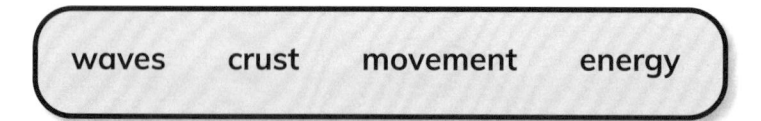

> waves   crust   movement   energy

An earthquake happens when there is a sudden _____ of rocks in the Earth's crust. This creates huge amounts of _____. The energy transfers into _____. The waves travel through the Earth's _____ to the surface.

b List **three** types of damage that result from earthquakes.

_____

_____

_____

c Which part of the world has the most earthquakes?

_____

4.3 Earthquakes

Practice

2

a   What is this huge sea wave called?

   _____

b   What causes it to happen?

   _____

   _____

c   Describe what will happen to this village.

   _____

   _____

4 Earth and its habitats

Challenge

3 There are millions of people who live in parts of the world at risk of earthquakes. Read about how some people have tried to reduce the damage caused by earthquakes, then answer the questions below.

> Many cities are built in areas where earthquakes often occur. Some of these cities, such as cities in Japan and California, in the USA, have special laws about building. The laws say that all new buildings must be built in a way to prevent them collapsing during an earthquake. Buildings must have deeper, stronger foundations (the concrete base a building is built on). This helps to absorb ground movements and reduce the effects of shaking.
>
> Animals such as dogs and birds behave strangely before earthquakes. Scientists think that animals can sense vibrations before an earthquake. For example, before a huge earthquake which occurred in China, many snakes came out of their winter sleep even though the weather was freezing cold.
>
> In high risk areas of China, people have been asked to tell the authorities if they think animals are behaving strangely.

a   How do cities in Japan and California try to prevent buildings being destroyed during an earthquake?

_____

_____

b   How do Chinese people in rural areas know when an earthquake is about to happen? Give an example.

_____

_____

_____

> ## 4.4 Different habitats

Focus

A

B

1 Look at Picture A.

   a Describe the habitat.

      _____

   b Identify the animal.

      _____

   c Describe **one** way that this animal is suited to its habitat.

      _____

      _____

4 Earth and its habitats

2 Look at Picture B.

   a Describe the habitat.

     _____

   b Identify the animal.

     _____

   c Describe **one** way that this animal is suited to its habitat.

     _____

     _____

Practice

3 Look at these pictures of the feet of different birds.

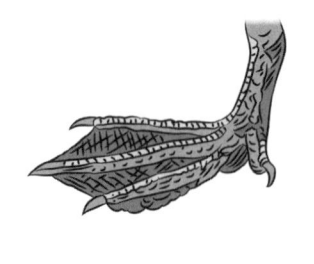

    A   B   C   D

   a Which bird do you think grips branches of trees?

     _____

   b Which bird do you think walks?

     _____

4.4 Different habitats

c Which bird do you think swims?

_____

d Give an example of a type of bird that swims.

_____

e Which bird do you think eats smaller birds and small animals?

_____

f Give an example of a type of bird that eats smaller birds and animals.

_____

Challenge

4 Read the text about giraffes, then answer the questions below.

> Giraffes live in the tropical grassland regions of Africa. It is hot and dry for most of the time. There is grass and trees have small leaves and thorns. Giraffes are suited to this habitat in various ways.
>
> There are other animals that eat the leaves off the trees and bushes lower down. But these animals are not as tall as the giraffe. The giraffe can eat the leaves at the tops of the trees.
>
> A giraffe has a long, thick tongue which it can curl around a branch and pull the leaves into its mouth. A giraffe's mouth is covered with very thick skin so the thorns don't hurt it. A giraffe's neck is three metres long! A giraffe has a very large heart because it has to pump blood all the way up this long neck to its brain!

4 Earth and its habitats

a   Describe the habitat the giraffe lives in.

_____

_____

b   How can the giraffe reach the leaves at the tops of the trees?

_____

c   Describe **two** ways in which the giraffe can eat leaves on thorny trees.

_____

_____

_____

_____

5 Light

> 5.1 How we see things

Focus

1 Arun is looking at a palm tree.

a Name the source of light.

_____

b Complete this sentence to show how Arun sees the tree.

Light travels from the _____ to the palm tree. The light

_____ off the palm tree into Arun's _____.

This is how Arun _____ the palm tree.

5 Light

Practice

2 Mrs Liong is sewing. She needs to see the needle she is trying to thread.

a Name the light source Mrs Liong is using.

_____

b Name the objects Mrs Liong is trying to see.

_____

c Sometimes Mrs Liong sits outside in her garden in the morning and sews. Describe how she sees her sewing.

_____

_____

5.1 How we see things

Challenge

3 Zara is looking for a box of books. She thinks the box is in the cupboard. It is very dark in the cupboard.

   a What is the object that Zara is trying to see?

   _____

   b Why can't Zara see the object in the cupboard?

   _____

   _____

   c What must Zara do to be able to see the object in the cupboard?

   _____

   d Explain how Zara will see the object when she follows your advice.

   _____

   _____

   _____

5 Light

> 5.2 Light travels in straight lines

Focus

1 Sofia and her friend Zara have a flexible plastic tube and a flashlight. Complete these sentences, which describe how they can use these things to prove that light travels in straight lines.

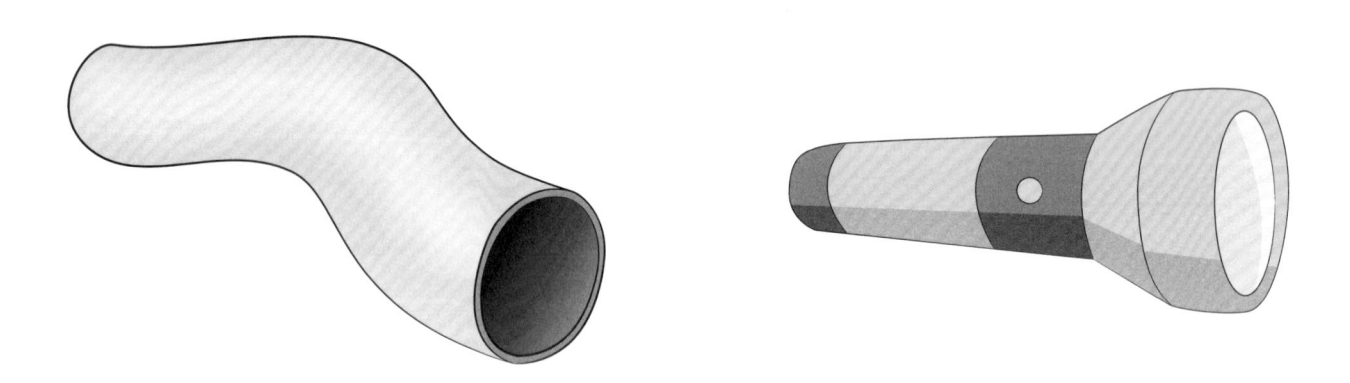

Sofia shines the _____ down the tube. Zara can see the

_____ when she looks down the tube from the other end.

Sofia makes a _____ in the tube.

She shines the flashlight down the tube again. This time Zara cannot see the light.

This demonstrates that light travels in _____ lines.

5.2 Light travels in straight lines

2 Arun is looking at a palm tree.

a Identify the source of light.

_____

b Draw rays to show how Arun sees the tree.
Label the arriving ray and the reflected ray.

Practice

3 Rabah and Khalid are walking along the corridor at school.
The corridor is lit by lamps in the ceiling.

Rabah is behind Khalid. Rabah can see Khalid.
But then Khalid turns the corner at the end of the corridor and Rabah cannot see Khalid anymore.

a What is the source of light in the corridor?

_____

b Fill in the spaces in these sentences to explain how Rabah can see Khalid:

Light shines on _____. Light _____ off Khalid

and travels into _____ eyes.

5 Light

c Explain why Rabah cannot see Khalid when Khalid has walked around the corner.

4 On the picture, draw rays to show how Mrs Liong sees her needle. Label the arriving ray and the reflected ray.

Challenge

5 Marcus is sitting under the table. His friend Sofia puts a can on top of the table.

'What have I just put on top of the table, Marcus?', asks Sofia.

'I don't know Sofia, I can't see on top of the table.'

Marcus can use a mirror. Then he will see what is on top of the table.

On the picture below, draw **three** rays to show how Marcus sees the can.

> 5.3 Light reflects off different surfaces

Focus

1 Zara is looking at her face in a mirror.

  a Describe the surface of the mirror.
     Choose from this list: dull, shiny, bumpy, smooth.

     _____

  b What name do we give to the reflection of Zara's face in the mirror?

     _____

  c Complete this sentence to explain how Zara sees her face in the mirror.

     Light shines from the _____ on to Zara's face.

     Light from Zara's face travels to the _____.

     The mirror _____ Zara's _____ into her eyes.

  d Why can't Zara see her face in a piece of wood?

     _____

5 Light

Practice

2 a What could Arun and Marcus use instead of a mirror – a sheet of aluminium foil or a wooden chopping board?

b Explain why you chose the surface you wrote in your answer to the previous question.

c How do you think people looked at their reflection before there were mirrors?

d Do all surfaces reflect some light? How do you know this?

5.3 Light reflects off different surfaces

Challenge

3 Mr Damsong is driving his car. He looks in his rear view mirror to see the cars coming behind him.

These events describe how the rear view mirror helps Mr Damsong to see what is behind him. But they are in the wrong order.

Write numbers 1–6 in the first column.
Number 1 describes the first event and Number 6 the last event.

Order of events	Event
	The light reflects off the car behind Mr Damsong.
	Mr Damsong sees the car behind him.
	The light reflects off the rear view mirror
	The light travels into Mr Damsong's eyes
	The light travels to the rear view mirror.
	Light from the Sun shines on the car behind Mr Damsong.

5 Light

> 5.4 Light in the solar system

Focus

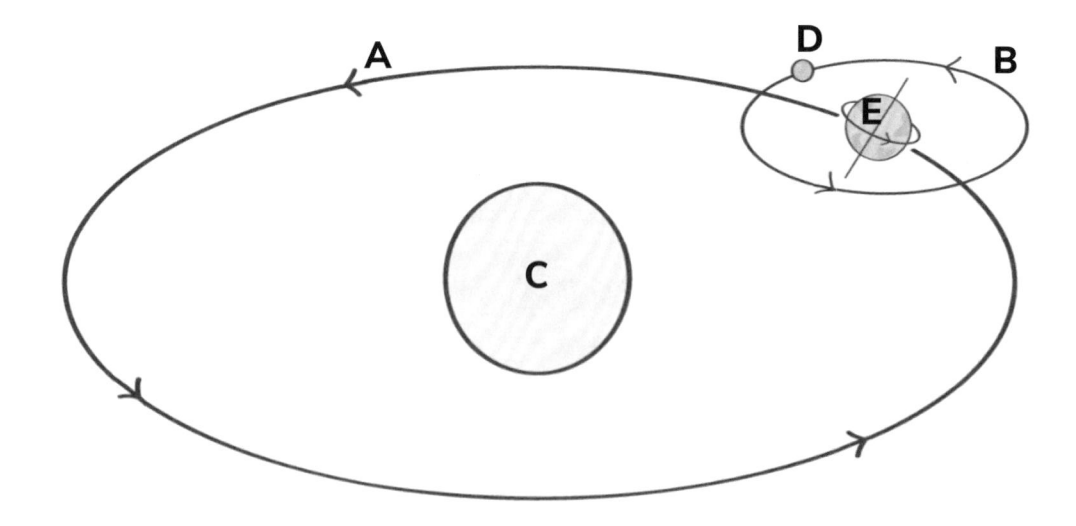

1 a Complete the table by filling in the second column.
You will find the letters on the diagram.

You will need to use some letters more than once.

The first one is done for you as an example.

	Letter on diagram
Moon	D
Sun	
Earth	
Orbit of the Moon around the Earth	
Orbit of the Earth around the Sun	
A planet	
A star	
A body in space that gives out light	
A body in space that reflects light	

5.4 Light in the solar system

b List the planets in the solar system beginning with the planet closest to the Sun.

_____

_____

c Write down **three** other types of body in the solar system besides a star and a planet.

_____

_____

_____

Practice

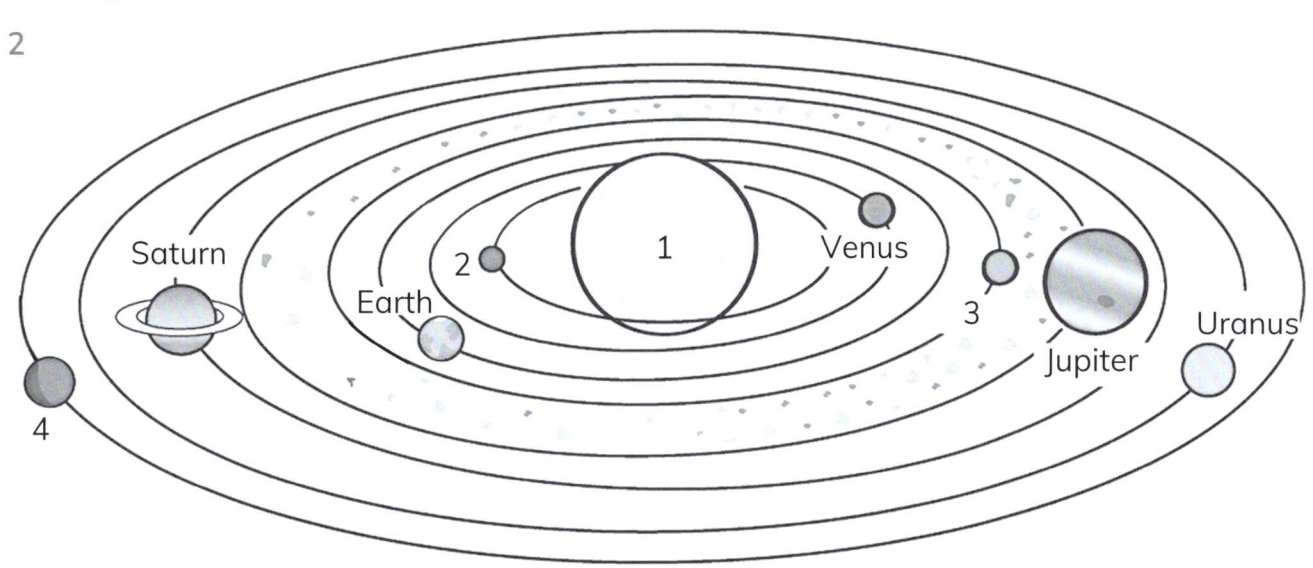

2

a What does this diagram represent?

_____

b Name the body labelled 1.

_____

5 Light

c   Name the planets 2, 3 and 4.

_____

_____

_____

d   How long does it take Earth to make one orbit around the Sun?

_____

e   Does Venus take a longer or a shorter time than Earth to make one orbit around the Sun?

_____

f   Explain your answer.

_____

g   Which planet takes the longest time to orbit the Sun?

Explain your answer.

_____

5.4 Light in the solar system

Challenge

3 Read how scientists have changed their ideas about planet Mars.

> Mars is often called the 'Red Planet' because it looks red in the sky. The ancient Romans called the planet Mars after the god of war. They associated the colour red with war.
>
> In the 17th century the telescope was invented. When you look through a telescope you see everything much larger. Scientists used telescopes to study Mars. They observed that Mars spins on its axis and they observed ice on Mars. They thought that people lived there. They called the people Martians.
>
> In the 19th century telescopes improved so scientists could observe more about Mars. They saw that Mars has two moons.
>
> In the 20th and 21st centuries many spacecraft have visited Mars. 'Rovers' have landed on Mars and sent back information about the rocks, the ice and the atmosphere (the air surrounding the planet). We now know that the red colour is caused by iron oxide in the rocks. Scientists now know that the atmosphere around Mars consists of carbon dioxide.

a What is Mars?

_____

b Is Mars closer to the Sun or further from the Sun than Earth is?

_____

c How does a telescope help scientists to observe the solar system?

_____

d How did people observe Mars before telescopes were invented?

_____

e What did the Romans know about Mars?

_____

5 Light

f Write down **two** things that scientists discovered when telescopes were invented.

_____

_____

g What information have scientists obtained recently that:

explains why Mars is red in colour?

_____

shows that people cannot be living there?

_____

> 5.5 Day and night

Focus

1 a On the diagram, label the Sun's rays and the Earth's axis and spin.

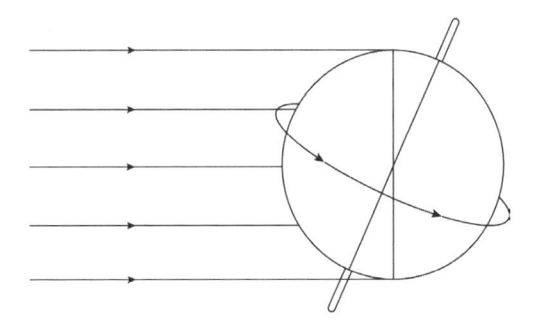

b How long does Earth take to spin once round its axis?

_____

c On the diagram, colour in the part of the Earth having night.

Practice

2 a Why does almost every part of the Earth's surface have some hours of daylight and some hours of darkness every day?

_____

_____

_____

b All the planets spin on their axes. Why do all the planets have some hours of daylight and some hours of darkness?

_____

5 Light

c   Mercury takes 59 Earth days to spin once round its axis.

Are the nights and days longer or shorter than on Earth?

_____

d   Jupiter takes 10 Earth hours to spin once round its axis.

Are the nights and days shorter or longer than on Earth?

_____

Challenge

3   Earth is one of the planets in the solar system. All the other planets spin on their axes, like Earth does. But they spin at different speeds. Look at the data in the table. Mercury takes 59 Earth days to complete one spin. This means one 'day' on Mercury would be like 59 days on Earth!

Planet	Time taken to complete one spin
Mercury	59 Earth days
Venus	243 Earth days
Earth	24 Earth hours
Mars	24½ Earth hours
Jupiter	10 Earth hours

a   When a planet spins on its axis, what does the half of the planet facing the Sun experience?

_____

5.5 Day and night

b Which planet has the longest 'day'?

_____

c If you lived on the planet with the longest day and slept for half the day, how long would you sleep for every day?

_____

d Which planet has the shortest day?

_____

e If you lived on the planet with the shortest day, how many hours would you be at school every day if, on Earth, you spend about 6 hours at school every day?

_____

5 Light

> 5.6 Investigating shadow lengths

Focus

1 The drawing shows the results of a shadow stick experiment.

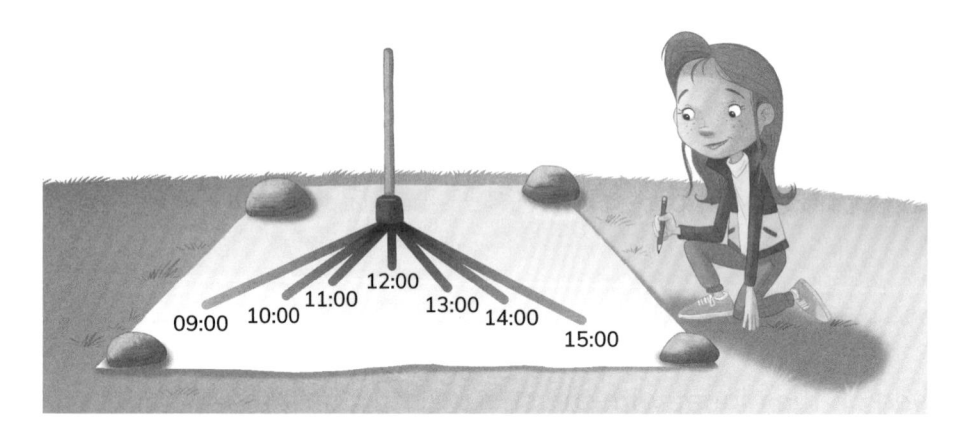

a At what time on the shadow stick does the Sun appear to be highest in the sky?

_____

b Does this result in a long or a short shadow?

_____

c At which times on the shadow stick does the Sun appear lowest in the sky?

_____

d Does this result in a long or a short shadow?

_____

e Describe the pattern in the lengths of shadows at different times of day.

_____

_____

5.6 Investigating shadow lengths

f Predict the length of the shadow at 18.00.

_____

Practice

2 Here is a diagram of a shadow stick experiment.
   Look at the position of the Sun at 09:00.
   A ray comes from the Sun and casts a shadow of the stick, labelled 09:00.

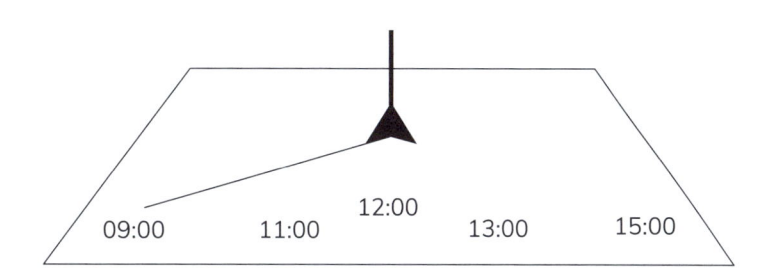

a On the picture, draw the positions of the Sun at 11:00, 12:00, 13:00 and 15:00.
   Then draw the shadows of the stick for each position of the Sun.

b What movement does the Sun appear to make between 09:00 and 15:00?

_____

_____

c Does the Sun really move how it appears to do?
   Explain your answer using your scientific knowledge.

_____

_____

5 Light

Challenge

3   Look at the pictures of a tree that are numbered 1–5.
    Each picture shows the Sun in a different position in the sky
    and the shadow is a different length.

    Drawing number 1 shows 08:00 in the morning.

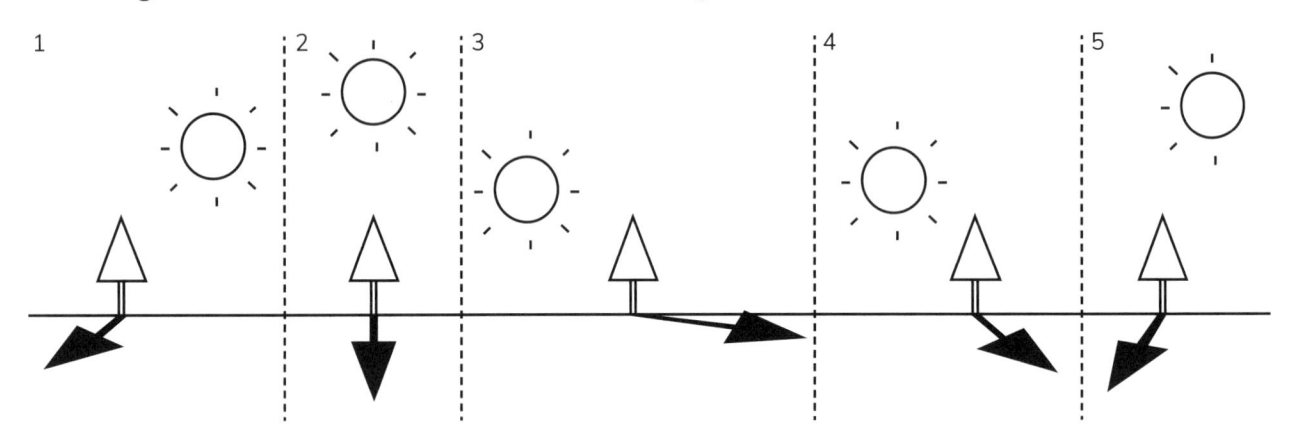

    a   Which drawing represents each of these times?

        10:00 _____

        12:00 _____

        16:00 _____

        19:00 _____

    b   Write down the **two** factors that you used to decide which drawing
        represented each time.

        _____

        _____

6 Electricity

> 6.1 Which materials conduct electricity?

Focus

1 a Complete this sentence:

   A material that allows electricity to pass through it is an electrical _____.

  b Write a similar sentence to explain what an electrical insulator is.

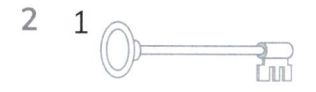

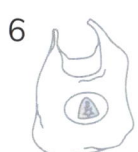

   _____

2 Identify the objects 1–6 in the picture.
   Now identify the material each object is made from.
   Fill in your answers in column 2 of the table.

   Decide whether each object is an electrical conductor or electrical insulator.
   Put a tick (✓) in either column 3 or column 4.

Object	Material object is made from	Electrical conductor	Electrical insulator
1			
2			
3			
4			
5			
6			

6 Electricity

Practice

3 a Predict whether the lamp will light up in each of the following circuits. Write 'Yes' or 'No' alongside each circuit.

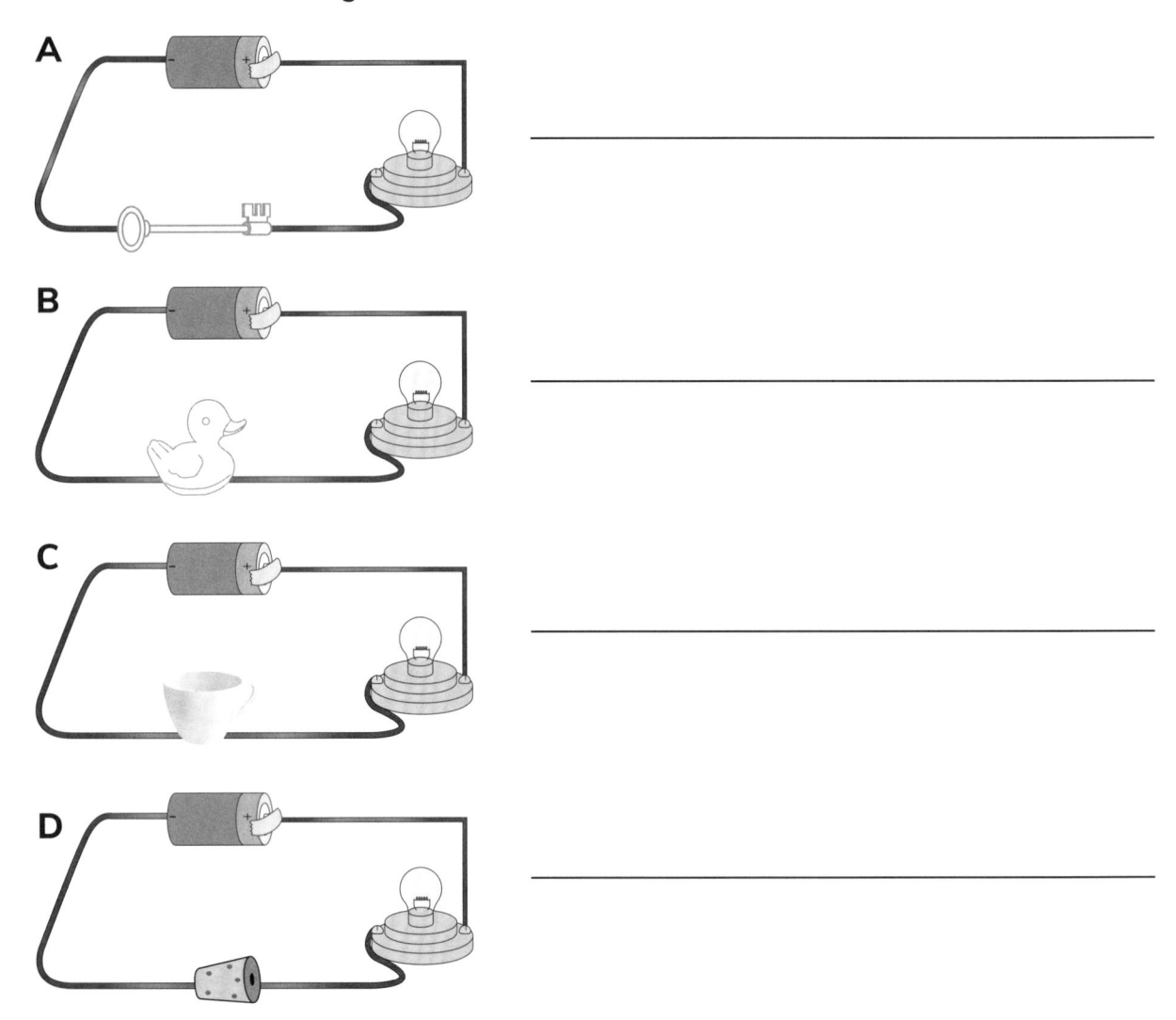

A _____

B _____

C _____

D _____

b Which materials (A, B, C or D) are electrical conductors and which materials are electrical insulators?

_____

_____

6.1 Which materials conduct electricity?

c   Complete the sentence below to make your conclusion.

   Materials made of _____, like the key, are electrical

   _____.

   Materials made of ceramic, plastic and cork are _____ of electricity.

Challenge

4 Sofia and Zara have made a circuit to test whether different objects are electrical conductors or electrical insulators.

   a   How can they test that their circuit works?

   _____

   _____

   b   They tested these four objects:

   coin   chopstick   glass   plastic spoon

   Predict which of the four objects will conduct electricity and which will not. Put a ✓ next to the objects that will conduct electricity, and a ✗ next to the ones that will not conduct electricity.

   c   How can Sofia and Zara test each object?

   _____

   _____

   _____

6 Electricity

d   What do Sofia and Zara conclude about which materials are electrical conductors and which are electrical insulators?

_____

e   Use your conclusion to predict whether each of the following objects will be conductors or insulators of electricity.

> a key   a glass bottle   a cork   a plastic spoon

Fill in your answers in the table.

Object	Material object is made from	Electrical conductor	Electrical insulator

84

> 6.2 Does water conduct electricity?

Focus

1 a What is pure water?

_____

b How is tap water different to pure water?

_____

c Why can plants, animals and humans conduct electricity?

_____

Practice

2 In the space below, design and draw a poster to put up in a restaurant kitchen. The poster must warn workers never to use electric stoves and appliances with wet hands.

Make sure your poster is eye-catching and has a picture that will make your message clear.

6 Electricity

Challenge

3 Jawad has just completed a 20 km run. He is very hot and sweaty.

The first thing he does when he gets home is turn on the electric fan. Jawad moves the fan and touches some bare connecting wire where the plastic insulation has worn away.

a What has happened to Jawad?

_____

b List **three** factors that caused this to happen:

A _____

B _____

C _____

> 6.3 Using conductors and insulators in electrical appliances

Focus

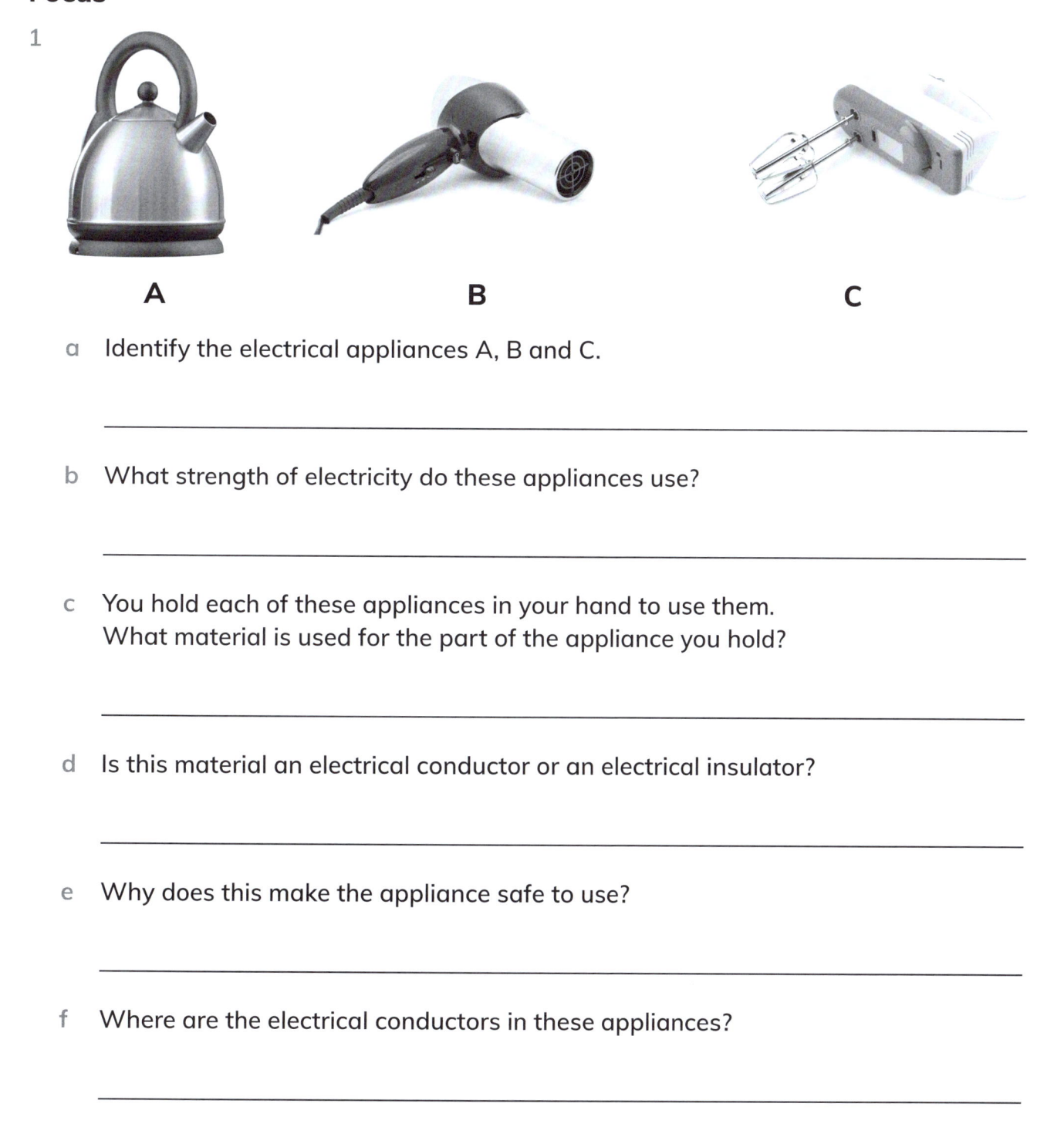

1.

       A   B   C

a   Identify the electrical appliances A, B and C.

___

b   What strength of electricity do these appliances use?

___

c   You hold each of these appliances in your hand to use them. What material is used for the part of the appliance you hold?

___

d   Is this material an electrical conductor or an electrical insulator?

___

e   Why does this make the appliance safe to use?

___

f   Where are the electrical conductors in these appliances?

___

6 Electricity

Practice

2 Here is a picture of a kitchen.

a Name the electrical appliance used in the picture.

_____

b Identify **two** dangers in using this appliance. Use these words in your answer:

> insulation   metal   conducts   electric shock   salts

_____

_____

_____

_____

6.3 Using conductors and insulators in electrical appliances

Challenge

3   The electricity for electrical appliances at home comes from big cables outside. You may have seen these cables strung from big structures called pylons like the photograph below. The pylons are made of metal.

There are lots of cables carrying the electricity. It is important to keep the cables apart. To do this they use ceramic separators. Ceramic is clay.
You can see these on the second photograph.

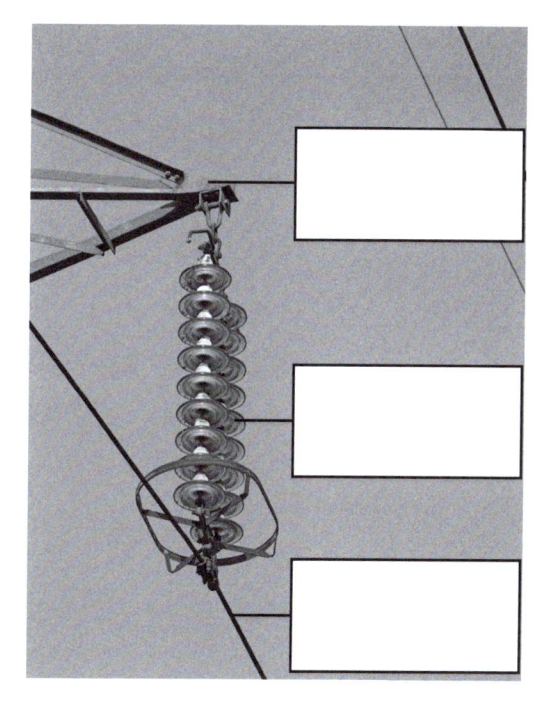

On the second photograph label '**pylon**', '**cable**' and '**ceramic separator**' next to the label lines.

a   Why are the cables made of metal?

_____

b   What type of metal do you think the cables are made from?

_____

c   Why are the separators made of ceramic?

_____

89

6 Electricity

4 Arun and Marcus are flying their remote control helicopter. The wind blows and the helicopter gets caught in the cables on a pylon.

'Let's climb up the pylon and get it back', says Arun.

Do you think they should do this? Explain your answer.

_____

_____

_____

> 6.4 Switches

Focus

1 a What does a switch do in a circuit?

   _____

   b Look at the pictures A and B.

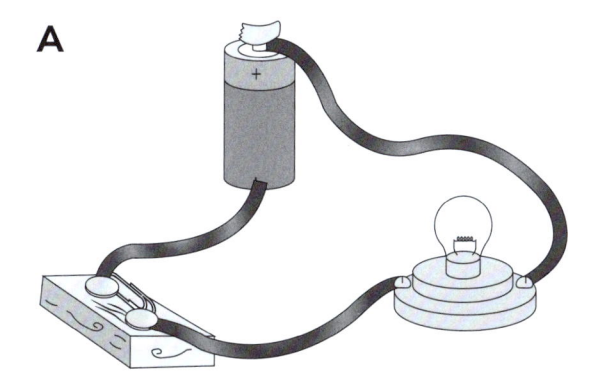

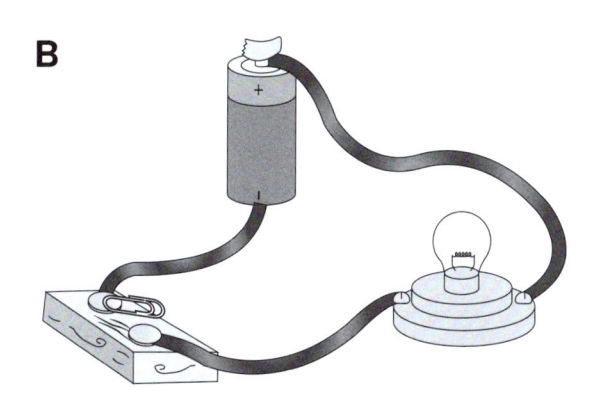

   A

   B

   In which of the two circuits, A or B, should the lamp light up? Explain your answer.

   _____

   _____

   _____

   c How can a switch cause a 'break in the circuit'?

   _____

   _____

   _____

6 Electricity

Practice

2   Look at circuits A and B.

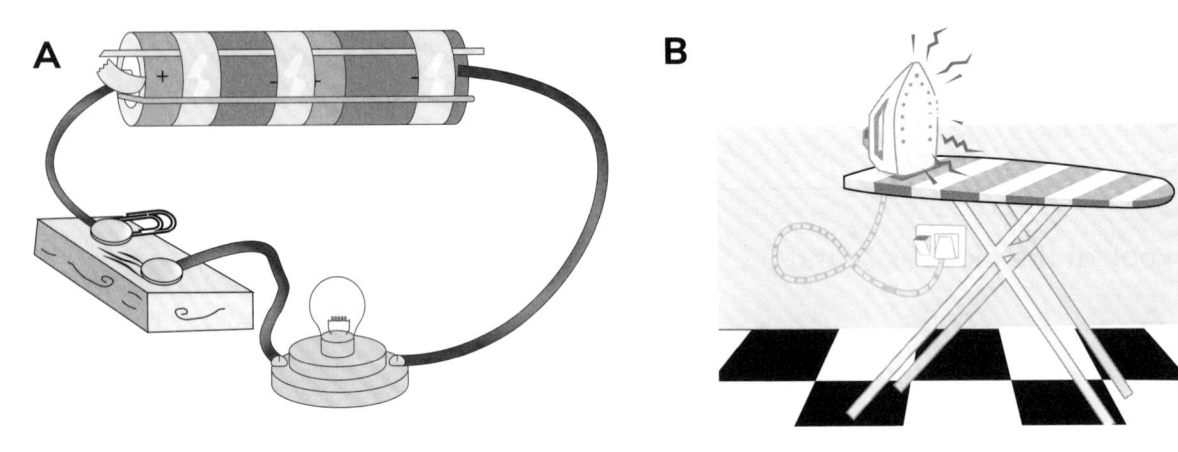

A

B

a   Predict if electricity is flowing in circuit A.

_____

b   Explain your answer.

_____

c   What must you do to circuit A to make the lamp light up?

_____

d   Predict if electricity is flowing in circuit B.

_____

e   Explain your answer.

_____

f   What must you do to circuit B to turn off the iron?

_____

6.4 Switches

Challenge

3 Zara and Marcus want to build a circuit with a lamp that shines brightly. They build circuit A.

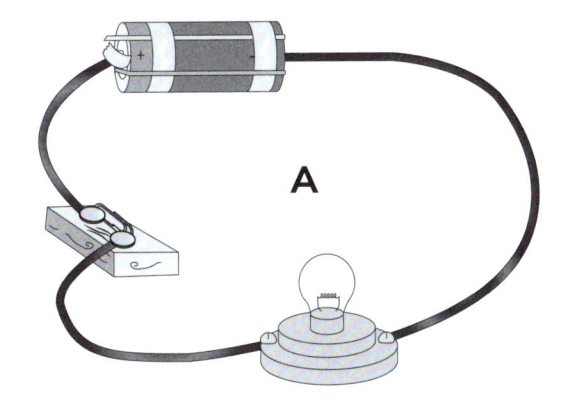

a Name the components that they used to make their circuit.

_____

_____

b How do you know that the circuit is closed?

_____

4 Look at circuit B. They added another cell to make the lamp brighter. But the lamp did not light up at all.

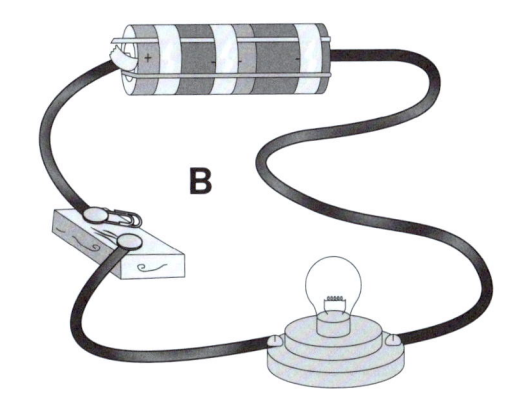

a Why did the lamp not light up?

_____

b What change must Zara and Marcus make to circuit B to make the lamp light up?

_____

6.5 Changing the number of components in a circuit

Focus

1.

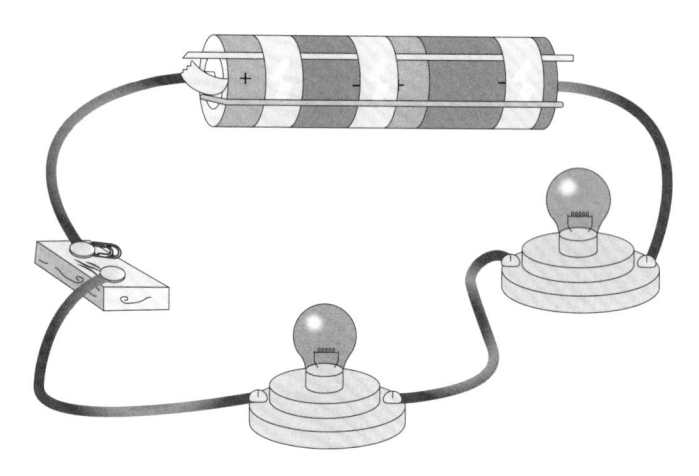

a List **five** components of the circuit.

___

___

___

___

___

b What must you do to the circuit before the lamps light up?

___

c You add another lamp to the circuit.
Do the lamps glow more brightly or less brightly?

___

6.5 Changing the number of components in a circuit

d   Explain your answer.

_____

_____

Practice

2

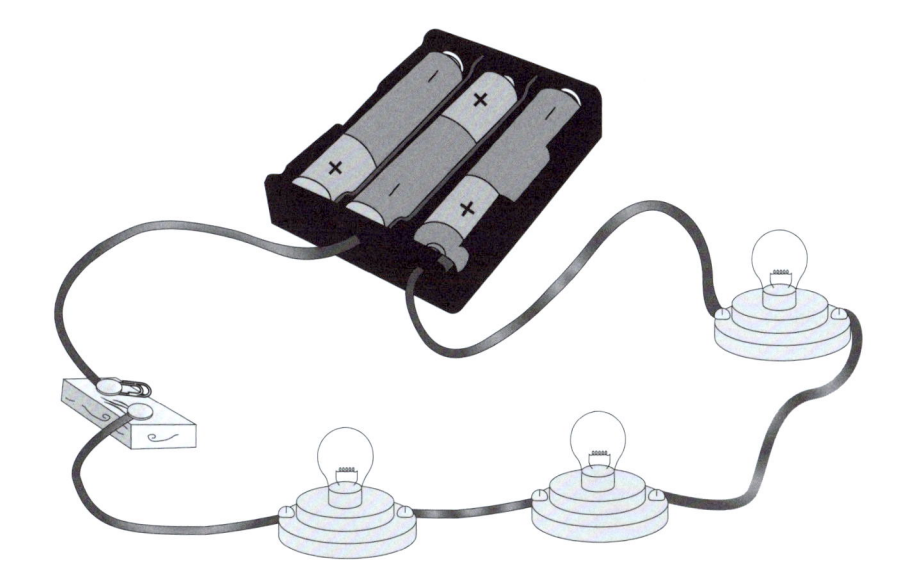

a   List the components in the circuit.

_____

b   Will the lamps light up? Explain your answer.

_____

c   If you remove a lamp from the circuit, will the remaining lamps glow more brightly or less brightly?

_____

d   If you add a lamp to the circuit, will the remaining lamps glow more brightly or less brightly?

_____

6 Electricity

e If you remove a cell from the circuit, will the lamps glow more brightly or less brightly?

_____

f If you add a cell to the circuit, will the lamps glow more brightly or less brightly?

_____

Challenge

3 a In the picture, (circle) the components you need to make a circuit with a 3V battery, two lamps in lamp holders and a switch.

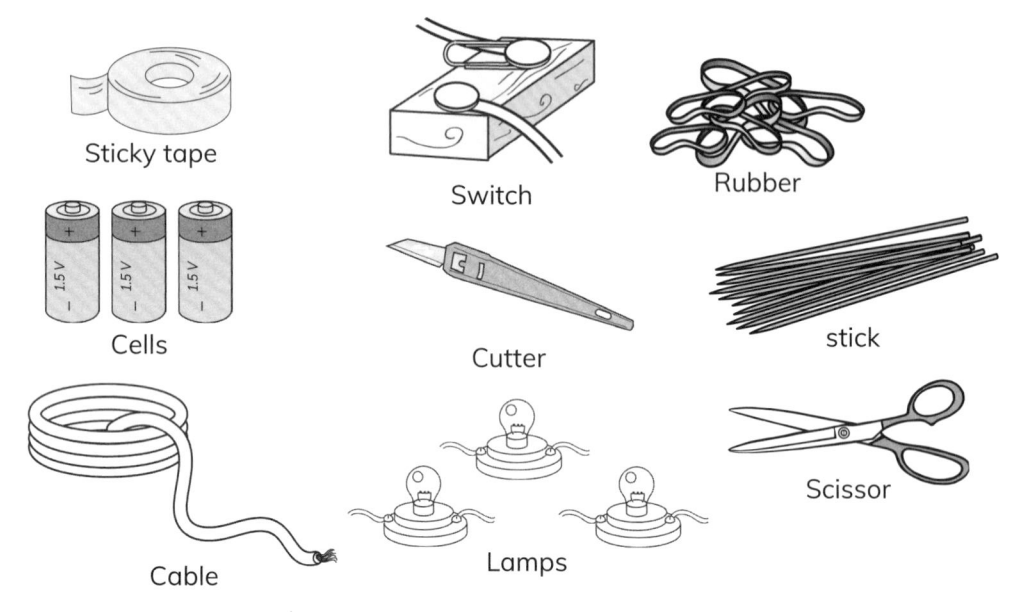

Sticky tape
Switch
Rubber
Cells
Cutter
stick
Cable
Lamps
Scissor

b What can you do to make a 3 V battery using the things in the picture?

_____

_____

6.5 Changing the number of components in a circuit

c   If you make the circuit, predict whether the lamps will come on.

_____

_____

d   Predict what will happen if you remove a lamp from the circuit.

_____

_____

e   Explain why you think this will happen.

_____

_____

f   Predict what would happen if you added a third lamp to your circuit.

_____

_____

g   Explain why you think this will happen.

_____

_____

Acknowledgements

The authors and publishers acknowledge the following sources of copyright material and are grateful for the permissions granted. While every effort has been made, it has not always been possible to identify the sources of all the material used, or to trace all copyright holders. If any omissions are brought to our notice, we will be happy to include the appropriate acknowledgements on reprinting.

Thanks to the following for permission to reproduce images:

Cover image by Omar Aranda (Beehive Illustration)

Unit 1: Rzdeb/GI; **Unit 2:** Vasiliki/GI; Santje09/GI; **Unit 3:** TEK IMAGE/GI; Buena Vista Images/GI; Roman Milert/GI; **Unit 4:** Sebastián Crespo Photography/GI; Beboy_ltd/GI; Haje Jan Kamps/GI; Ig0rZh/GI; Robert Postma/GI; Rmbarricarte/GI; Mirrorimage-NL/GI; **Unit 5:** Motion picture library/Paul Ridsdale/Alamy; Shulz/GI; Vchal/GI; SDI Productions/GI; **Unit 6:** Mikroman6/GI; Adam Gault/GI; Cris180/GI; Pioneer111/GI; Jose A. Bernat Bacete/GI; Stefano Carnevali/Shutterstock; Hwangdaesung/GI.

Key: GI= Getty Images.